PATHS TO DESTRUCTION

A Group Portrait of America's Jihadists—
Comparing Jihadist Travelers with
Domestic Plotters

Brian Michael Jenkins

RAND
CORPORATION

For more information on this publication, visit www.rand.org/t/RR3195

Library of Congress Cataloging-in-Publication Data is available for this publication.
ISBN: 978-1-9774-0560-9

Published by the RAND Corporation, Santa Monica, Calif.
© Copyright 2020 RAND Corporation
RAND® is a registered trademark.

Cover design by Peter Soriano

Support RAND
Make a tax-deductible charitable contribution at
www.rand.org/giving/contribute

www.rand.org

Preface

Ever since the September 11, 2001, terrorist attacks, homegrown jihadist terrorists have been a major security concern for the U.S. government. In this report, I examine hundreds of U.S. residents who have traveled or attempted to travel to foreign lands to join or otherwise support foreign terrorist organizations. The focus of the analysis is on the individuals' characteristics and what their collective demographic profile can reveal about who is going abroad to join jihadist groups. The research outlined here furthers analysis described in my 2017 piece titled *The Origins of America's Jihadists*.

The observations derived from this continuing research should be of interest to government analysts and policymakers, as well as other researchers, academics, and members of the general public who seek to better understand jihadist radicalization and recruiting in the United States.

Funding

Funding for this report was provided by gifts from RAND supporters and income from operations. RAND's research findings and recommendations are based on data and evidence and therefore do not necessarily reflect the policy preferences or interests of its clients, donors, or supporters.

Contents

Figures and Tables

Prologue

This report describes information about U.S. residents identified as engaging in conduct that is considered terrorism under U.S. law; specifically, the report examines those traveling abroad or attempting to do so in order to join and fight for, or support in other ways, foreign terrorist organizations. These individuals are often called *foreign fighters*. However, they are *foreign* only from the point of view of the terrorist organizations based outside the United States. Likewise, they are often labeled as foreign fighters by the U.S. counterterrorism experts for whom the terrorist organization is the principal framework of analysis.

In the United States, however, these individuals are not *foreign* fighters but Americans who have joined or sought to join a foreign terrorist organization. My primary interest in this study is not in their contribution to such an organization as fighters; rather, I am interested in the individuals themselves and what their collective demographic profile can reveal about who is going abroad to join jihadist groups.

Moreover, of the hundreds of Americans (and thousands from other countries) who are labeled as foreign fighters, not all went abroad with the intention of fighting in jihadist formations. For example, some who went to Syria in the early years of the civil war there did so to join the rebellion against the Syrian government. They were not jihadists—at least not initially; as the conflict evolved, however, they might have joined or been swept into jihadist groups. Still others went abroad to provide humanitarian assistance to the rebels. Some went simply to live in and help build the caliphate declared by the leader of the Islamic State of Iraq and Syria; thus, they served a supporting but not a fighting role. And some were brought along by husbands or parents. Therefore, in this report, I use the broader term *traveler* to refer to these individuals. The nature of their involvement in the jihadist cause is a variable.

This report should be read as a companion to an earlier RAND Corporation publication, *The Origins of America's Jihadists,* which focused on those who, inspired by jihadist ideology, carried out or plotted terrorist attacks in the United States.[1] This report updates that earlier work and allows the comparison of travelers with *plotters*—those who were inspired by jihadist ideology to carry out or who plotted to carry out terrorist attacks in the United States—and the examination of both as a single group.

A third installment, currently in preparation, will address those who were arrested in the United States for providing jihadist organizations with other kinds of assistance, such as financing, arms and other materiel, recruiting, and the dissemination of terrorist propaganda.

The three pieces together are intended to provide a comprehensive group portrait of America's jihadists.

For Whom This Report Is Written and Why

I hope that the observations derived from this research will offer insights to government analysts and policymakers and will assist other researchers, academics, and members of the general public in increasing the understanding of jihadist radicalization and recruiting in the United States—an issue of continuing concern.

But why am I compiling this information? Many people may assume that the government publishes such data and wonder why the report does not simply cite the definitive government sources. Such an assumption would be wrong.

In testimony before the Senate Homeland Security and Governmental Affairs Committee shortly after the Fort Hood, Texas, shooting in 2009, I noted that, since the terrorist attacks on September 11,

---

[1]   Brian Michael Jenkins, *The Origins of America's Jihadists*, Santa Monica, Calif.: RAND Corporation, PE-251-RC, 2017.

2001, authorities in the United States had "uncovered nearly 30 terrorist plots involving 'homegrown terrorists.'"[2] In the short time between the invitation to testify and the date of the hearing, I was unable to find a government source that compiled the attacks, plots, arrests, and names of individuals. My statement that there were nearly 30 plots derived from my own quick review of accounts in the news media.

Following the hearing, I was surprised at the interest expressed by both government officials and others in my hastily compiled chronology, which was surely incomplete. Certainly, somewhere in government, I thought, there must be a comprehensive chronology of terrorist attacks, interrupted plots, arrests, and prosecutions. These are public events. The U.S. criminal justice system is a matter of public record.

From the mid-1980s until 2005, the Federal Bureau of Investigation published unclassified annual reports on terrorist activity in the United States, including attacks, arrests, and disruptions.[3] It no longer does so. The U.S. Department of Justice issues press releases for individual arrests, but these cover only those arrested for federal crimes. In 2017, the National Counterterrorism Center began publishing a list of jihadist terrorist attacks in the United States.[4] In other words, although the information can be retrieved, it is not consolidated or complete.

The National Counterterrorism Center's list does not include terrorist plots; therefore, compiling such data has been left to researchers outside of government, and the details included are thus more controversial. There is no consolidated list of individuals charged, some of whom may be prosecuted in state rather than federal courts, and none of the government publications provides complete biographical information on the individuals.

---

2   Brian Michael Jenkins, "Going Jihad: The Fort Hood Slayings and Home-Grown Terrorism," testimony presented before the Senate Homeland Security and Governmental Affairs Committee on November 19, 2009, Santa Monica, Calif.: RAND Corporation, CT-336, 2009.

3   The last of these was Federal Bureau of Investigation, *Terrorism 2002–2005*, Washington, D.C.: U.S. Department of Justice, 2006.

4   National Counterterrorism Center, *Foreign Terrorist Inspired, Enabled, and Directed Attacks in the United States Since 9/11*, McLean, Va., January 2019, Not available to the general public.

Government possession of data does not always lead to the data's analysis. The analysis of counterterrorism understandably tends to focus on tactical and operational developments. Investigators devote themselves to current cases. Analysts are driven by the latest threats. Thus, additional analysis that looks at broader pools of data and explores trends does not occur with much regularity.

Compilations of data and the analysis of them may also raise unwelcome questions about policy. Ideally, policy should derive from analysis, but that is not always the case. Often, policy decisions reflect the latest events filtered through the political views of the policymakers. Chronologies of events, headcounts of terrorists, and other forms of empirical evidence might paint a picture that differs from the policymakers' narrative and can thus be problematic for the policymakers.

For whatever reasons, the federal government has affirmatively chosen not to provide the public with a comprehensive accounting of terrorist activity in the United States, and that decision is not because withholding the information serves the interests of national security: The data in this report are not classified. In fact, the data exist in the public domain, just not in a single place or in a readily accessible way.

The data-gathering, compilations, and analysis reflected in this report and previously published work are intended to add to what is still a small body of research on the American jihadist phenomenon and provide information that members of the public, and perhaps even some counterterrorism practitioners, might not know.

Summary of Key Judgments

A Measure of Success

U.S. counterterrorism efforts include not only military operations abroad but also an intensified international and domestic intelligence effort and a robust law enforcement campaign against America's jihadists at home. Although deadly attacks have occurred in the United States, the domestic counterterrorist campaign can claim a measure of success.

Between the terrorist attacks of September 11, 2001 (9/11), and December 2019, there were no terrorist attacks conducted by jihadist terrorists deployed in the United States from other nations.[1]

Overall, authorities have uncovered more than 80 percent of the known jihadist terrorist plots in the United States before the attack could be carried out.

Jihadist activity in the United States has consisted mostly of thwarted plots or one-off attacks carried out by a single individual or, in a few cases, a handful of individuals. All the attackers have been arrested or are dead.

There is no known organized jihadist underground in the United States, there are no unsolved terrorist crimes, and no organized jihadist groups capable of continuing a terrorist campaign have emerged.

---

[1] However, on December 6, 2019, a Saudi aviation student opened fire on U.S. personnel at the Naval Air Technical Training Center in Pensacola, Florida. Investigators subsequently discovered that he had embraced jihadist ideology as early as 2015 and had ties with al Qaeda before coming to the United States (Eric Tucker, "FBI: Shooter at Pensacola Navy Base Coordinated with al-Qaida," *Military Times*, May 18, 2020). Because this event occurred after this report was being prepared for publication, it is not reflected in this analysis.

Of the 422 American jihadists identified in this research, including those who carried out or plotted terrorist attacks in the United States since 9/11 or who sought to travel to jihadist fronts abroad, more than 70 percent have been sent to prison, where most remain.

Sixty-three of the American jihadists are known to be dead: Fifteen died in attacks in the United States or were killed in subsequent shootouts with police, 47 were killed abroad, and one died from a drug overdose after returning to the United States.

The U.S. legal system has worked. Apart from two individuals who were held in military custody for years before being turned over to the civilian courts, the defendants associated with terrorism have been charged with crimes, have maintained their civil rights, and were brought to trial before a judge or a judge and jury who could independently assess the evidence and decide whether the person was guilty. Of those who were tried, almost all were convicted.

Profile of the Travelers

Of the 422 American jihadists, 280 were travelers or would-be travelers. Their average age was 25 years. Ninety-three percent were men.

More than half of the travelers were born in the United States. Most of those who were born abroad arrived in the United States as children and spent an average of 11 years in the country before attempting to join a jihadist group abroad, which suggests that they radicalized while in the United States.

With the exception of Somali Americans who went to Somalia following Ethiopia's invasion of that country in 2006, most of the travelers were not returning to their ancestral homelands. Only eight of the 145 travelers who headed to Syria or Iraq were originally from one of those countries.

Syria's civil war offered a unique confluence of appeal and accessibility. More than half of the identified travelers left the United States after 2011, almost all heading for Syria and wanting to join the Islamic State of Iraq and Syria (ISIS).

There have been no similar flows to other less-accessible or less-inviting jihadist fronts, such as Afghanistan in the 1980s; the Balkans in the 1990s; or South Asia, East Africa, and the Middle East after 9/11 but prior to the rise of ISIS in 2014.

Of the 280 Americans who were publicly identified or arrested for traveling or attempting to travel to jihadist fronts overseas, 81 (29 percent) were intercepted by law enforcement before they left the United States, and 48 were intercepted on the way, simply failed to connect with a group, or backed out and returned to the United States (three are unknowns).

The interception rate has significantly improved: Of the 116 pre-2012 travelers, only 14 (12 percent) were arrested before departing the United States, compared with 75 (46 percent) of the 164 travelers attempting to depart in 2012 or later.

The Threat Posed by Returning Travelers

As of February 2019 (when the data for this report were collected), 43 identified travelers might still be at large. (There may be others who are believed to have left the United States but who have not been publicly identified.) Given that some of these 43 people were last reported to have been in Yemen, Syria, or Iraq—intense conflict zones—as long as ten years ago, some of them were probably killed there.

All travelers face arrest upon their return to the United States. Any who might successfully sneak back into the country would have to remain in hiding to avoid detection. Contact with family, friends, or fellow jihadists could expose them to arrest.

Those sympathetic to the jihadist cause are also likely to suspect that returning travelers not in custody are free only because the authorities are watching them or have already recruited them as informants.

Some returnees, however, could remain determined to carry out attacks. And some may have acquired specialized skills while abroad—for example, bomb-making—that render the returnees especially dangerous.

However, the deadliest jihadist terrorist attacks that have been carried out in the United States since 2013 did not require advanced skills, only access to firearms or vehicles, and were perpetrated by individuals who had neither traveled overseas nor received guidance from other extremists domestically or abroad.

The Travelers Compared with the Plotters

The research confirms that a frustrated desire to travel abroad can be an indicator of willingness to carry out attacks at home.

When comparing those who sought to travel with those who plotted attacks but did not attempt or indicate a desire to travel, I find more similarities than differences.

The plotters and the travelers are similar in that approximately half of the individuals in both sets were born in the United States and half were born abroad.

Those born abroad spent roughly the same number of years in the United States before taking some kind of action or being arrested, suggesting that both the foreign-born travelers and the foreign-born plotters radicalized while in the United States.

The travelers were, on average, four years younger than the plotters—25 versus 29 years old. This could reflect that younger people have a greater willingness to leave the United States or that the social media recruiting campaign of ISIS reached a younger audience.

The travelers included a greater number of women, although that difference was almost exclusively connected to ISIS. Only one woman (excluding a wife arrested for lying to protect her husband) was involved in a plot to carry out a terrorist attack in the United States; she joined her husband in carrying out the mass shooting in San Bernardino, California, in 2015. Neither she nor her husband traveled overseas to join al Qaeda or ISIS prior to the attack. (Several returning women were not prosecuted.)

The Travelers and Plotters Combined

Some individuals opted to leave the United States to join jihadist groups abroad to defend the Muslim community against what they saw as infidel aggression, while others decided to carry out attacks in the United States. Combining the travelers and plotters gives us an overall profile of these individuals.

The average age of the combined group at the time of first travel or arrest for plotting, attacking, or attempting to travel abroad was 27; the median was 25. (In this report, all reported *averages* are means, and medians are typically reported also.)

America's jihadists have been overwhelmingly male; about 6 percent were women, and most of those traveled or attempted to travel to Syria.

About half of the 422 identified jihadists were born in the United States; 205 were verified to be U.S.-born, and available information suggests that another 14 were also born in the United States, accounting for 52 percent of the total. This is a somewhat higher percentage than that reported for the plotters (48 percent) in a related 2017 study, described in *The Origins of America's Jihadists*.[2]

Of the 187 American jihadists who were born outside the United States, more than half were naturalized U.S. citizens, and roughly one-third were lawful permanent residents. Only 12 were in the United States on temporary visas; four entered the country illegally (three of these came in 1984 as small children with their families).

Information available for 112 of the 187 foreign-born plotters and travelers shows that most entered the United States as minors and spent an average of 12 years between arrival and either first attempt to travel or arrest for plotting, attacking, or attempting to travel abroad to join a jihadist group. This finding is the same as that in the earlier study of plotters only.[3] The finding suggests that America's jihadists do not reflect an immigration problem; that is, it does not appear that radical-

---

[2] Brian Michael Jenkins, *The Origins of America's Jihadists*, Santa Monica, Calif.: RAND Corporation, PE-251-RC, 2017.

[3] Jenkins, 2017.

ized individuals are being admitted into the United States or that vetting is failing. America's jihadists are made in the United States.

America's foreign-born jihadists came from at least 48 countries. Somalia leads the list with 31, followed by Pakistan with 25. Muslim-majority countries dominate the list, but 14 of the jihadists (7 percent) came from Balkan countries (including Albania); 17 came from Latin American and Caribbean countries. Apart from the unique Somali experience, national origin was a poor indicator of future terrorist activity.

Using information available for 273 individuals, it appears that the education level of America's jihadists is not significantly different from the education level of the general U.S. population. And using educational achievement as a rough marker for socioeconomic status, plus anecdotal evidence, suggests that America's jihadists come from diverse socioeconomic backgrounds. Thus, radicalization does not seem to be a product of poverty or deprivation.

Information on whether the jihadists were born into the Muslim faith or later converted was available for 358 of the 422 individuals. In this study, 35 percent of the 358 individuals were converts; in the earlier analysis, 38 percent of the individuals examined were converts.

Beginning in 2014, there were sharp increases in the number of terrorist plots in the United States and the number of attempts to travel abroad. These increases were driven by ISIS's efforts to recruit foreign fighters and others who wished to live in a caliphate, the group's success on the ground in the Middle East, its terrorist attacks in the West that captured global attention, and the group's steady drumbeat of propaganda encouraging attacks by lone actors.

The peak year for travelers was 2014, with a significant decline in 2016, and the peak year for terrorist attacks and plots in the United States was 2015, with a significant decline in 2017. One potential explanation for these numbers peaking at different times is that, as ISIS came under intense military pressure, travel to Syria became less attractive and more dangerous, persuading would-be travelers to contemplate terrorism at home instead. The destruction of the Islamic State territory also invited revenge.

When the final territory held by ISIS was recaptured in 2019 by the Syrian government and other partners fighting to defeat the group, it did not end the terrorist threat. The lure of jihadist ideology will continue to attract recruits, particularly individuals suffering personal crises. However, without an easily accessible destination and a recruiting draw, the number of American travelers will likely revert to the smaller numbers seen in the years before the Syrian civil war.

Acknowledgments

Many readers might not appreciate how much labor is required, even in an age of internet-assisted research, to compile the information and assemble a database of more than 400 individuals. There is no single source. Often, the information sought—citizenship status, dates of entry into the United States, whether an individual is a convert to the Muslim faith—is not easily accessible, is contradictory, or is simply unavailable. Fortunately, in the preparation of this report, I was able to rely on the dedicated assistance of Anita Szafran, who became master of the constantly revised spreadsheets used to support the findings. I am extremely grateful for her dedication and diligence in what often appeared to be a Sisyphean task. I also want to thank my RAND Corporation colleague Heather J. Williams, who generously shared the data used in her related research project.

The report has also benefited from research in this field by Peter Bergen, Bennett Clifford, Karen Greenberg, Seamus Hughes, Charles Kurzman, Alexander Meleagrou-Hitchens, John Mueller, Mitchell D. Silber, and Anne Speckhard.

Rigorous review is a requirement of RAND research. Again, I was fortunate to have as my reviewers two individuals with long frontline government experience in dealing with this topic: Javed Ali's review reflected his nearly two decades in government, serving with the Federal Bureau of Investigation (as senior national intelligence officer), the National Counterterrorism Center, and the National Security Council. Richard C. Daddario is a former federal prosecutor and later deputy commissioner for counterterrorism at the New York Police Department. Both went far beyond the traditional role of a reviewer, and their thorough and thoughtful reviews assisted me enormously in clarifying my conclusions and marshalling the supporting evidence.

In addition to the formal reviews, David Lubarsky, a friend and RAND donor, patiently read through multiple drafts. We agreed that the potentially contentious nature of the subject matter and my conclusions would expose the report to determined, even hostile, readers. David raised questions and pointed out where further explanations were needed.

The report is a complicated read, heavy with statistics. It benefited greatly from the always skillful editing of Janet DeLand, who has assisted me for more than three decades in communicating the results of my research. I also wish to thank John Godges, who reviewed the hundreds of entries in the traveler data set to provide an additional check on accuracy, and Allison Kerns for her detailed review of the final numbers in the text and charts and additional editorial suggestions. I am also grateful to Saci Detamore, who provided the original conceptualization of the graphics that visually portrayed the findings, helped prepare the report for the publication process, and kept it moving through those steps.

Finally, I wish to express my gratitude to the RAND Corporation for the corporate support of my independent research and, in particular, to Michael Rich, RAND's president and chief executive officer, for his continuing personal encouragement and support over many years.

CHAPTER ONE

Introduction

The leaders of the contemporary armed jihadist movement in such groups as the Islamic State of Iraq and Syria (ISIS) and al Qaeda have sought to create a global enterprise by disseminating their ideology to a worldwide audience via the internet, assembling alliances, acquiring affiliates or so-called provinces, and colonizing local combatant groups. They have sought to enlist foreign recruits and exhorted homegrown jihadists to carry out terrorist attacks. This effort has been going on for decades, but it has intensified since 2014. To what degree have the jihadists succeeded in the United States? And what threat does their presence pose to homeland security in the future?[1]

In a 2017 RAND piece, *The Origins of America's Jihadists*,[2] I examined the profiles of 178 individuals who, motivated by jihadist ideology, carried out or plotted terrorist attacks in the United States between the terrorist attacks of September 11, 2001 (9/11), and May 2017. For

---

[1] These questions have been part of a continuing corridor of my research at the RAND Corporation. Publications include Brian Michael Jenkins, *Stray Dogs and Virtual Armies: Radicalization and Recruitment to Jihadist Terrorism in the United States Since 9/11*, Santa Monica, Calif.: RAND Corporation, OP-343-RC, 2011; Brian Michael Jenkins, *When Jihadis Come Marching Home: The Terrorist Threat Posed by Westerners Returning from Syria and Iraq*, Santa Monica, Calif.: RAND Corporation, PE-130-1-RC, 2014; Brian Michael Jenkins, *Inspiration, Not Infiltration: Jihadist Conspirators in the United States*, testimony presented before the House Oversight and Governmental Reform Committee on December 10, 2015, Santa Monica, Calif.: RAND Corporation, CT-447, 2015; and Brian Michael Jenkins, *The Origins of America' Jihadists*, Santa Monica, Calif.: RAND Corporation, PE-251-RC, 2017.

[2] Jenkins, 2017.

the study described in the present report, I have added 18 individuals who plotted attacks between June 2017 and April 2019 or who plotted attacks earlier but were not identified in the first analysis; these 18 bring the total number of attackers and plotters to 196 (see Appendix B).

Defining Travelers

In Islam, migrating from the land of disbelievers to the land of God is referred to as *hijrah*. Those who make this journey are called *muhajirun* (emigrants), and they are praised by the Prophet. In this report, I focus on U.S. residents (native-born and naturalized citizens, lawful permanent residents, and other long-term residents) who have traveled or attempted to travel abroad to join jihadist fronts; I refer to these individuals as *travelers*. Between 9/11 and February 2019,[3] there were 280 U.S. residents who were publicly identified or arrested for traveling or attempting to travel abroad to join or support terrorist organizations. Because 54 of the travelers were also attackers and plotters, the total combined number of people covered in this report and the previous RAND piece is 422. The 54 who fall into both categories are included in the analysis of travelers' collective profile but should not be double-counted when the two sets are combined.

The U.S. residents whom I refer to as travelers are often called *foreign fighters*. However, they are *foreign* only from the point of view of the terrorist organizations based outside the United States. That term was introduced during the Syrian civil war to describe the thousands of volunteers from many countries who traveled to Syria primarily to join the jihadist forces fighting against the Syrian government. The term has continued to be used as some of these people return to their home countries.

---

[3] In this report, I looked for anyone who was *identified or arrested* for traveling or attempting to travel between September 11, 2001, and February 2019, as noted. Some of those individuals actually *traveled* as early as 1989, and the last arrest for a traveler in the data set is October 2018. The data in the spreadsheet included as a supplement to this report were current as of February 2019 (see Appendix A).

One of the main reasons that I use the term *traveler* instead of *foreign fighter* is that, of the hundreds of American travelers, not all went abroad to fight at the side of the jihadists. For example, some went to provide humanitarian assistance to the beleaguered people of Syria and only later became fighters; jihadist recruiting appeals deliberately blurred the line between aid and action. Others traveled abroad to live in the newly established Islamic State or to seek husbands there. Some were children brought along by their families. Of course, some of these individuals shared the radical ideology of the jihadists and provided material support for designated terrorist organizations. And, in some cases, the jihadists recruited children for participation in atrocities and military operations. Sorting out and dealing with the population of returnees is a complicated problem, especially in Europe, where the number of travelers vastly exceeds the number from the United States.

A future study in this series will examine the Americans who were arrested in the United States for providing some type of assistance—for example, financial assistance, military materiel, or training—to jihadists at home or abroad but who neither traveled abroad nor plotted terrorist operations in the United States. The three groups examined in the three studies constitute a comprehensive portrait of America's jihadists.

Objectives of the Research

Because fewer than 200 individuals fell into the category of homegrown attackers and plotters considered in the earlier study,[4] the first objective with this updated study was to simply increase the total number of American jihadists examined. Adding the travelers more than doubles the number examined earlier and therefore leads to greater confidence in the overall conclusions suggested in the analysis.

The second objective was to compare the travelers with those who plotted or carried out attacks in the United States. Are there significant

---

[4] Jenkins, 2017.

differences in their demography or backgrounds that propelled some to go abroad or instead join the armed jihad at home?

In this analysis, I also compare the earlier travelers—those who went abroad before 2012 to join al Qaeda or the Taliban in Afghanistan or al Shabaab in Somalia or to seek training from jihadists in Pakistan—with the later travelers, who traveled primarily to Syria and Iraq in 2012 or thereafter. In addition, I compare those who joined ISIS with those who more recently joined other jihadist formations. The appeal of ISIS was based on a combination of the group's message, its military successes on the ground, its creation of a caliphate, and its extensive use of social media to reach a broader audience. But did it attract a different set of volunteers as a result?

A current U.S. security concern is that travelers returning home from jihadist fronts, especially Iraq or Syria, will carry out terrorist attacks in the United States or use their jihadist credentials to attract others and form new homegrown terrorist groups. As of this writing, none of the returnees from Syria had carried out a terrorist attack in the United States or been arrested for plotting to carry out an attack. The few that were known to have returned had been arrested for providing material support to a terrorist organization.

To assess the threat posed by returnees from Syria, I examined the historical record of previous returnees in an analysis published in 2014.[5] At that time, only a small number of individuals who went to Syria had been identified. The present report may be considered an expansion and replication of that earlier work, and, for convenience, some portions of the earlier report are repeated here. In this study, I also look for additional clues in the European experience, although the numbers and circumstances of jihadist returnees in Europe are very different from those in the United States (see box on the following pages).

---

[5]   Jenkins, 2014.

The Situation in Europe Is Different

Both al Qaeda and ISIS exhorted supporters abroad to carry out attacks in the countries where they lived, but al Qaeda, under intense assault after 9/11, did not attract many fighters to Afghanistan. Other al Qaeda fronts attracted some volunteers from neighboring countries, but few were Westerners. In contrast, ISIS successfully recruited individuals, including Westerners, to travel to its territory and fight for the cause.

An estimated 40,000 people traveled to Syria to join or support the fight; some estimates put the figure at 50,000.

Most of these travelers came from surrounding Arab countries, but approximately 5,000 European residents traveled to Syria. Not all were fighters and not all fighters initially intended to join ISIS. Some came before the emergence of ISIS to join the rebellion against the Syrian regime or to provide humanitarian aid. Given the organizational chaos and fluid loyalties that characterized rebel forces, some who started out in the more secular rebel formations ended up, by circumstances or choice, in the jihadist fronts that came to dominate the opposition forces.

Citizens of four countries—France, Belgium, Germany, and the United Kingdom—accounted for more than 70 percent of the Europeans traveling to Syria.

Whereas traveling to join jihadist fronts in Syria or elsewhere was considered a crime in the United States, not all European countries initially viewed it that way, and few efforts were made to intercept travelers. Attitudes began to change when ISIS-linked attacks, especially in France and Belgium, were carried out by returning travelers associated with local confederates. In the aftermath of the November 2015 attacks in Paris and the March 2016 attack in Brussels, returning travelers came to be regarded as a major terrorist threat.

Those two attacks, however, were the work of a single network led by a second-generation Belgian-Moroccan and reflected unique situations in those countries. Other attacks in France that occurred after November 2015 were not connected to that same network and fell more into the province of homegrown plots.

Of the Europeans who traveled abroad to join jihadist fronts, about 30 percent had returned to their home countries by 2016. As of this writing, the returnees had not produced the wave of terror that many feared, although a few returning fighters were involved in terrorist attacks. Perpetrators also included some would-be travelers and failed asylum seekers. At the same time, there had been numerous home-grown attacks by individuals with no foreign travel experience.

Debate continues among Europeans about how to deal with the returning travelers. Some countries have adopted the U.S. approach and want to send these individuals to prison. Supporters of that approach fear that trying to keep all of these individuals under surveillance in a free society would overwhelm resources and that, when subsequent terrorist attacks occur, authorities would be blamed. Others in Europe reject the idea that all travelers should be incarcerated. Instead, supporters of this alternative approach are looking for ways to de-radicalize and reintegrate the travelers into society while also supervising them to some degree to help reduce the risk of local attacks.

SOURCES: Bérénice Boutin, Grégory Chauzal, Jessica Dorsey, Marjolein Jegerings, Christophe Paulussen, Johanna Pohl, Alastair Reed, and Sofia Zavagli, *The Foreign Fighters Phenomenon in the European Union: Profiles, Threats & Policies*, The Hague: International Centre for Counter-Terrorism, April 2016; and Anthony Dworkin, Beyond *Good and Evil: Why Europe Should Bring ISIS Foreign Fighters Home*, London: European Council on Foreign Relations, October 25, 2019.

CHAPTER TWO

A Brief History of Americans Leaving to Fight Abroad

U.S. citizens leaving the United States to join foreign armies or rebel forces abroad is not a new phenomenon. Over the past 200 years, tens of thousands of Americans not affiliated with the military have traveled abroad to fight on foreign soil.

Fighting Overseas: From Mexico to Greece

For example, hundreds of Irish American and other European Catholic immigrants deserted the U.S. Army to fight on Mexico's side during the war with Mexico in 1847.[1] In 1865, many former Confederate soldiers, including some Confederate generals, fled to Mexico instead of surrendering to the Union. Some accepted the invitation of Emperor Maximilian I to join the Mexican Imperial Army, and others went to establish Confederate colonies.[2] Their presence prompted increased official U.S. support for the Mexican rebels, led by Benito Juárez.

In 1911, several hundred U.S. citizens crossed the border to participate in the Mexican Revolution. A mixed force of Mexican rebels and U.S. citizens, many of them anarchist members of the Industrial Workers of the World hoping to create a socialist utopia in Mexico,

---

[1] Francine Uenuma, "During the Mexican-American War, Irish-Americans Fought for Mexico in the 'Saint Patrick's Battalion,'" *Smithsonian Magazine*, March 15, 2019.

[2] J. Fred Rippy, "Mexican Projects of the Confederates," *Southwestern Historical Quarterly*, Vol. 22, No. 4, April 1919.

defeated the Mexican garrison in Baja California and for several months held the cities of Tijuana and Mexicali before government forces drove the forces off.[3]

In 1912, as many as 25,000 Greek Americans responded to Greece's call for volunteers to fight the Ottoman army during the Balkan Wars. This was no secret exodus: With American sentiments on their side, the volunteers held fundraisers and marched in parades. Running for president at the time, Woodrow Wilson wished them well and promised to welcome them back. The New York National Guard sold them uniforms and equipment and helped train them.[4]

Prior to the United States' entry into World War I in 1917, hundreds of Americans ignored official U.S. neutrality and volunteered to join the French, British, and Canadian forces.[5] Thousands more joined the armed forces of Canada and the United Kingdom between 1939 and December 1941, before the United States joined World War II. Some Americans may have served with the German Army during that war, but the reported number is far fewer than the number of those who joined the fight against Germany.

Between 1936 and 1939, more than 30,000 foreign volunteers, including an estimated 2,800 Americans, fought in Spain's civil war, overwhelmingly on the side of the republic.[6] Because the United States remained officially neutral, the volunteers went secretly, but their participation was well publicized and widely popular as an opening battle in the fight against fascism. Later, during the Cold War, however, fighting for the Spanish Republic or even having a relative who did

---

[3]   Brian Michael Jenkins, *The Border War: A Study of United States-Mexico Relations During the Mexican Revolution 1910–1920*, Los Angeles, Calif.: University of California at Los Angeles, master's thesis, 1964; and Bob Owens, "Mexican Revolution and the Role Played by Tijuana," *San Diego Reader*, February 25, 1988.

[4]   Terry Stavridis, "The Greek-Americans and Balkan Wars 1912–13: Helping the Old Homeland," *Macedonian Studies Journal*, Vol. 1, No. 2, 2014, pp. 133–162.

[5]   "American Volunteers Entered World War I Early," Voice of America, February 18, 2015.

[6]   Adam Hochshield, *Spain in Our Hearts: Americans in the Spanish Civil War, 1936–1939*, New York: Houghton Mifflin Harcourt, 2016. See also Caleb Crain, "Lost Illusions: The Americans Who Fought in the Spanish Civil War," *New Yorker*, April 11, 2016.

so came to be viewed as evidence of potential Communist sympathies and a cause for suspicion in the United States.

More than 1,000 Americans volunteered to join Israeli forces during the Israeli War of Independence in 1948. Many of the volunteers were recently returned veterans of World War II who brought needed military experience and skills, especially to Israel's nascent navy, air force, and armored units.[7]

Joining Jihad: A 40-Year Phenomenon

With the assistance of the United States, Saudi Arabia, and Pakistan, thousands of foreign volunteers (estimates vary between 10,000 and 35,000) joined the Afghan insurgency against Soviet occupation in the 1980s.[8] Many of these fighters were ethnic Pashtuns living nearby in Pakistan. However, others came from more-distant, mostly Arab countries. The United States supported the Afghan resistance, and Central Intelligence Agency personnel were deployed to the region. In addition, perhaps several hundred private U.S. citizens traveled to Afghanistan. This is a rough estimate. Although there was a more or less organized pipeline to facilitate travel, there was no effort to systematically identify who was going or to count them.

Most of the foreign volunteers, collectively referred to as the *Afghan Arabs*, went home when Soviet forces withdrew in 1989, but others went on to fight in the Balkan Wars of the 1990s or to launch insurgencies in their own countries. Some of the most determined volunteers were later absorbed into al Qaeda.

Only two individuals in the database assembled for this research had gone to Afghanistan before 9/11. The first, Daniel Patrick Boyd, joined Afghan insurgents fighting against the Soviet-backed Afghan government in 1989. Because he did not arrive in Pakistan until Octo-

---

[7]   Yaacov Markovitzky, *Machal: Overseas Volunteers in Israel's War of Independence*, Jerusalem: Israeli Ministry of Education, 2007.

[8]   Maria Galperin Donnelly, Thomas M. Sanderson, and Zack Fellman, *Foreign Fighters in History*, Washington, D.C.: Center for Strategic and International Studies, 2017.

ber 1989 and the Soviet withdrawal was completed in February 1989, Boyd did not directly engage in combat against Soviet forces. However, the insurgency against the Afghan government left in place by the Soviets continued until the government fell in 1992. The second individual, Christopher Paul, traveled to Afghanistan in 1990. He trained with al Qaeda and fought with Afghan insurgents and later with jihadists in Bosnia during the Balkan Wars. Both Boyd and Paul were subsequently arrested in the United States for plotting terrorist attacks there. As of the time of this writing, they were both serving prison sentences.

From the beginning of its campaign, al Qaeda sought to awaken true believers throughout the Muslim world, arguing that it was their personal duty to join the group's jihad. During the late 1990s, thousands of foreigners arrived in al Qaeda's and other jihadist organizations' training camps in Afghanistan. Those traveling from Western countries likely did so mostly as individuals. An example of this cohort is U.S. citizen José Padilla, who traveled to Afghanistan in early 2001, trained at an al Qaeda camp, and returned to the United States with the intention of carrying out terrorist attacks. He was arrested upon his return home in 2002. As mentioned, there is no consolidated information on how many Americans went to Afghanistan during this period. And after 9/11, the veterans of those jihadist organizations scattered, some of them to pursue jihads in their home countries.

Several hundred travelers—mainly from Egypt, Syria, Sudan, Saudi Arabia, and Jordan, and a handful from the West—joined the insurgents during the U.S. occupation of Iraq that began in 2003. During the early 2000s, al Qaeda and its Yemen-based affiliate, al Qaeda in the Arabian Peninsula (AQAP), focused their communication efforts on inspiring homegrown terrorism, with some success. They also remained intent on attacking the U.S. homeland. The number of jihadist-inspired attacks and plots in the United States hit a high point in 2009, leveled, declined from 2012 to 2014, and then soared again in 2015. The number of jihadist travelers also declined in 2009 and 2010 but then began to climb again starting in 2012.

The conflicts in Libya and Yemen in the 2010s attracted very few travelers seeking to join or support the fights. Instead, Syria became the primary destination for foreign volunteers, for several reasons. At the outset of the Arab Spring, the rebellion against Basher al-Assad's government in Syria seemed to signal the end of another Middle Eastern dictator. Public opinion in the West generally sided with the rebels, especially as the Syrian government's response to the uprising became increasingly brutal. Western governments were also inclined to support the rebellion, although this support began to decline with growing fears that a post-Assad Syria would succumb to the same kind of chaos that had followed the overthrow of the Muammar Qaddafi regime in Libya; mounting worries about the growing jihadist role in the Syrian insurgency; and, at least in Washington, the fear that the United States would be dragged into another Middle East war.

Meanwhile, the number of people heading for Syria to join the fight there, including thousands from the West, soared. U.S. intelligence estimates put the total number of foreign volunteers who underwent training in Osama bin Laden's camps in Afghanistan between 1996 and the September 11, 2001, attacks somewhere between 10,000 and 20,000.[9] By 2016, the U.S. State Department estimated that more than 40,000 volunteers had gone to Syria.[10]

Among the jihadist formations in the Syrian rebellion, ISIS became the primary draw. It had momentum. It fought off its challengers in Syria and then, in 2014, swept across northern Iraq in a series of apparent military victories that, in reality, reflected the Iraqi Army's disintegration. ISIS's declaration of a caliphate put it on the map—literally. New contingents of foreign volunteers headed for Islamic State territory.

As noted earlier, the United States supported the flow of volunteers to the Afghan resistance in the 1980s, and it lacked efforts to intercept U.S. citizens heading to Afghanistan in the 1990s. In the post-9/11 environment, however, U.S. authorities were concerned about any new gatherings of American jihadists abroad. Travelers were now subject to

---

[9] National Commission on Terrorist Attacks upon the United States, *The 9/11 Commission Report*, Washington, D.C., 2004, p. 67.

[10] Justin Siberell, "Country Reports on Terrorism 2015," special briefing, Washington, D.C.: U.S. Department of State, June 2, 2016.

the material support provisions of anti-terrorist legislation, which made it a crime to even attempt to join a foreign terrorist organization.

Intensified efforts to prevent American jihadists from departing to Syria and a U.S.-led campaign to destroy the Islamic State—at least its territorial expression—closed off what may have been a safety valve for would-be travelers. These individuals then turned their efforts inward to plotting attacks in the United States, which likely led to the increase in homegrown plots in 2015. Russia took a different approach: Instead of criminalizing attempts to travel abroad to join terrorist organizations, Russian authorities reportedly saw travel to Syria as a way to rid the Caucasus of jihadist fanatics and thus facilitated the jihadists' departure to Syria.[11] Although the increase in homegrown U.S. plots could be attributed to efforts to keep would-be travelers at home, it is also possible to interpret the increase as a response to ISIS appeals, which turned into a revenge motive as the caliphate was reduced.

Ultimately, the U.S. government began to condemn travelers based on the side they fought on, not the act of going abroad to fight. The difference between the travelers identified in this report and most of the previous cohorts of volunteers serving in foreign military formations is that jihadist ideology dictates that the travelers are at war with the United States. The U.S. government would not have considered those who fought alongside the Mujahidin against Soviet invaders in Afghanistan in the 1980s to be foreign fighters or travelers. However, those who have traveled abroad in more-recent years have come under investigation for counterterrorism purposes. This group includes those who went to Somalia to join al Shabaab prior to February 2008, when the United States officially declared it to be a foreign terrorist organization. Those who joined nonjihadist rebels in fighting the Assad government in Syria or who served with Kurdish and Arab units that, with U.S. support, were fighting against ISIS also face questioning upon their return to the United States.

---

[11] Maria Galperin Donnelly, Thomas M. Sanderson, Olga Oliker, Maxwell B. Markusen, and Denis Sokolov, "Russian-Speaking Foreign Fighters in Iraq and Syria," Center for Strategic and International Studies, December 29, 2017.

CHAPTER THREE

Diverse Reasons for Joining Jihad

The statistical profiles compiled in this report reveal little about the motives of those categorized as jihadists. These individuals joined or sought to join jihadist fronts abroad for a variety of reasons. The period of travel examined here covers nearly three decades, during which circumstances and appeals changed. The earliest travelers went to fight Soviet invaders. Later cohorts joined groups in Pakistan. Somali Americans initially went to fight Ethiopian invaders. The most-recent travelers were drawn to Syria by the resistance to the Assad regime or were attracted by the announcement of a new caliphate.

My earlier review of those arrested in the United States since 9/11 for carrying out or plotting attacks on behalf of jihadist ideology, including attempts to join jihadist fronts abroad, showed equal diversity in motives.[1] Ideology was a common feature. The American jihadists described in the earlier study, like those examined here, often explained their actions as an expression of religious faith—in particular, their acceptance of and commitment to the ideology of armed jihad as an individual duty for all Muslims, as well as their determination to defend their native country against foreign invaders, defend all of Islam against infidel aggression, or punish attacks by Western infidels. Feelings of humiliation—personal and vicarious—and victimization, as well as the need to restore honor, also frequently appear in their accounts.

Ideology alone, however, does not fully explain the jihadists' decisions. People enter the realm of armed jihad for many reasons, includ-

---

[1]   Jenkins, 2017.

ing a yearning to participate in an epic struggle, a thirst for adventure, and the desire to prove oneself as a warrior. Many of the would-be jihadists appear to have been pulled in by a powerful desire to belong to something, which they could fulfill by plotting to carry out a terrorist plot in the United States, joining a jihadist group abroad, or providing some other form of support.

Potential jihadist volunteers were not recruited in the traditional sense. In the terrorist groups of the 1970s and 1980s, volunteers who signaled their readiness to participate in violence were joining a clandestine organization. Those already underground had to be careful who else they trusted to bring in. As in any criminal conspiracy, potential recruits were often relatives, former schoolmates, and individuals known to the terrorists for a long time. They were observed and vetted before being inducted. Groups were wary of infiltrators or unreliable individuals whose inadequate motivation, substance abuse problems, mental disorders, or other behavioral issues could imperil operations, tarnish the group's reputation, or expose it to betrayal.

After 9/11, jihadist organizations increasingly used the internet to recruit foreign volunteers, especially those in the West. ISIS went further and effectively exploited social media to reach an even broader audience. Many of the travelers, like many of the participants in terrorist plots, started their journey on the internet, although personal contacts also played an important role. Both al Qaeda and ISIS employed some of the same recruiting themes, such as continuing infidel aggression against Islam, the suffering of the believers, and the personal duty of all Muslims to take up arms in defense of the community. The events of the day—the Soviet occupation of Afghanistan, the Balkan Wars in the 1990s, the U.S.-led invasions of Afghanistan and Iraq early in the 21st century, and the brutal assault on Sunni rebels in Syria's civil war—underscored the recruiting themes.

Like previous cohorts of fighters, jihadist travelers were motivated by religious beliefs or political ideology. And like many young men, they were also attracted by adventure and the opportunity to participate in an epic contest to demonstrate their own courage and prowess as warriors.

Both al Qaeda and ISIS justified and exhorted followers to commit violence, but ISIS advertised atrocities as evidence of its authenticity and operational prowess. In addition, ISIS defined its enemies more broadly to include Muslims who did not share its extreme interpretation of Islam. Since the early days of the insurgency in Iraq, this had been a source of contention between al Qaeda and the more ruthless leadership of ISIS's organizational predecessors. ISIS media productions were filled with videos of beheadings, crucifixions, people being burned alive, and mass executions. Disturbing to most people, these images may have resonated with a different set of individuals, some of whom may have been more attracted by the appeal of unlimited violence than by the motivating ideology.

RAND research shows that the more-recent jihadist recruits have tended to be more weakly connected to the foreign terrorist organizations and their political goals, and, in many cases, there was suspected mental illness.[2] Some law enforcement officials have suggested that ISIS recruiters deliberately targeted the mentally disturbed, although it is not clear how the recruiters might identify or diagnose such people.[3] Although the jihadist volunteers were perhaps vulnerable, it does not appear that they were been beguiled or brainwashed; rather, they seemed eager to join the battle, and the animus came from within. Personal crises figure prominently in their biographies. Many of the travelers addressed here and the terrorist plotters addressed in earlier research could be described as alienated, drifting, troubled souls. Some clearly were dissatisfied with their lives and sought new identities. Embracing an extremist ideology that demands obedience—submission and strict rules for every aspect of life—placed their fate in the hands of God and relieved them of difficult decisions. This is the attraction of all extremist belief systems. The deliberate savagery

[2] Heather J. Williams, Nathan Chandler, and Eric Robinson, *Trends in the Draw of Americans to Foreign Terrorist Organizations from 9/11 to Today,* Santa Monica, Calif.: RAND Corporation, RR-2545-OSD, 2018.

[3] Rukmini Callimachi and Catherine Porter, "Toronto Shooting Rekindles Familiar Debate: Terrorist? Mentally Ill? Both?" *New York Times,* July 25, 2018.

that ISIS publicized reinforced and legitimized internal feelings of anger and aggression.

But ISIS had an additional attraction. The 2014 declaration of a caliphate by the group's emir, Abu Bakr al-Baghdadi, generated excitement among Salafi-jihadist Muslims worldwide. Here, at last, was the restoration of the long-awaited Islamic State that would go on to conquer the world for Islam. Coming at the crest of ISIS victories, Baghdadi's audacious assertion seemed to carry weight.

Some recruits came to the Islamic State as pilgrims, escaping what they considered to be the oppression of residing among infidels, to live among like-minded believers and build the new province of faith. Others came to fight in the ranks of the Islamic State's forces, perhaps to participate in the final battle between Muslims and nonbelievers, which is prophesized in Sunni eschatology. For others, hostility to what they saw around them was the primary drive. Reaching a distant jihadist front was not just a means of escaping their situations, building a new society abroad, or defending their religion. They wanted to gain the expertise and battle experience that would equip them to return and seek revenge on their enemies at home.

Whether the volunteers plotted to participate in terrorist plots in the United States or sought to join jihadist fronts abroad seems to be as much a matter of happenstance as the result of careful calculation. Some saw their participation as sequential—carry out an attack in the United States and then go abroad, or go abroad to gain the skills necessary to carry out an attack in the United States. Participation was the objective, and the form it took was often determined by chance.

Individual travelers seeking to connect with the Taliban or al Qaeda in Afghanistan might be viewed with suspicion (as potential infiltrators, for example), but these groups were in remote areas that were more or less under their own control. And those seeking to connect with jihadist groups in Syria during the civil war could join the groups' military formations in open battle. By 2014, ISIS operated as a sovereign entity, ruling a large swath of territory. These were not clandestine urban terrorist organizations whose members still pretended to live normal lives and were in touch with the outside world. Volunteers who showed up in border towns or at jihadist camps posed less risk to al Qaeda or ISIS than such volunteers did to the secret terrorist groups of earlier decades. Upon arrival, volunteers were more easily isolated and controlled, unable to leave without permission. The large number of foreign volunteers reaching al Qaeda in the 1990s or ISIS after 2014 could be treated as a commodity to be sorted out according to capabilities. Talent was spotted and exploited. Some arriving volunteers could be recruited for terrorist operations in their home countries. Poor-quality recruits could be assigned to menial support tasks. Those with mental problems could be sent on suicide missions.

The important thing is that there is no evidence that anyone was rejected as unsuitable. (However, it is entirely possible that volunteers considered suspicious or useless were simply murdered.) As a result, the population of travelers available for study had varied backgrounds and intentions. For example, the fact that individuals with histories of aggression, substance abuse, and mental health problems appear so prominently in the traveler population could reflect remote recruiting via the internet and social media, the violent messaging of ISIS, or the possible deliberate recruitment of mentally unstable individuals. But it also could reflect the fact that all comers were accepted, regardless of their abilities or motives. This is also true for the terrorist plotters whose status as jihadist warriors could be conferred after their attacks.

It is difficult to determine to what degree an individual might be motivated by ideology versus mental illness, and the two are not mutually exclusive. Just because someone has a history of mental problems does not mean that he or she cannot also be a jihadist. At the same time, one cannot automatically categorize every mentally disturbed Muslim as a jihadist. Weighing motivations when both elements are present is beyond this analysis.

It is impossible to know how many volunteers dropped out of the jihadist organizations, and I do not have any way of profiling such people. Thus, the database compiled for this report contains only the most-fervent, most-determined actors who, for whatever constellation of reasons, decided to travel from the United States to jihadist fronts abroad. The resulting profile, then, is one of extremists.

CHAPTER FOUR

Profile of the Travelers

As noted earlier, between 9/11 and February 2019, 280 U.S. residents were publicly identified or arrested for traveling or attempting to travel abroad to join or seek military training from jihadist organizations. However, there are likely more than that. For example, in 2015, U.S. authorities estimated that 250 Americans had gone just to Syria to fight.[1] A later estimate put the total at 300 for travelers to Syria and Iraq.[2] Only some of these individuals have been publicly identified and thus appear in the database that was compiled for this report. In addition, the numbers are murky: The reported figure of 250 Americans is said to include those known to have departed, as well those arrested before departure or by authorities in other countries on the way. The number of travelers who ended up in the ranks of jihadist formations in Syria is lower.

Of the estimated 250 Americans who traveled or attempted to travel to Syria to support jihadist organizations, I was able to identify only 144. Of these, 131 joined or intended to join the ranks of ISIS, while 13 others joined or intended to join Jabhat al-Nusra (al Qaeda's affiliate in Syria) or one of the other jihadist formations there. (In addition, there are five others who indicated that they wanted to join ISIS

---

[1] James B. Comey, "Threats to the Homeland," testimony presented before the Senate Committee on Homeland Security and Governmental Affairs, Washington, D.C.: U.S. Department of Justice, October 8, 2015.

[2] Alexander Meleagrou-Hitchens, Seamus Hughes, and Bennett Clifford, *The Travelers: American Jihadists in Syria and Iraq*, Washington, D.C.: George Washington University, February 2018.

fronts in other countries.) The U.S. government's estimate of 250 is an all-in number that includes those who successfully traveled, those intercepted before departure, and several who discussed their aspirations to go to Syria but either were arrested on other charges before leaving or simply decided not to go for other reasons. If the estimate of 250 is indeed close to the actual number who went or tried to go to Syria, there may be about 100 travelers to Syria who have not yet been publicly identified.

Including these still unidentified travelers in my database would increase the theoretical grand total to nearly 400 travelers, or roughly 20 per year when spread over a couple of decades. That would double the number of travelers since 2012 that have been identified for this report and would heighten the already sharp spike in the number of travelers between 2012 and 2016. The volume of those going to Syria appears to have declined dramatically since 2016.

The U.S. government possibly knows the identity of at least some additional travelers but does not want to make that information public and thereby warn those returning that they have been identified; they are on watch lists, not wanted posters. There also may be sealed indictments of individuals known to have been in the ranks of jihadist organizations, and, if the jihadists return, authorities could use such indictments as incentives for the travelers to become informants. Some may already be cooperating. Thus, domestic Islamists might be suspicious of any jihadist veteran telling Syrian war stories.

At the same time, there might be other unidentified travelers who left the United States in secret and either died overseas or remain at large—possibly even in the United States.

Of the travelers included in the database, all were identified or arrested for actions after 9/11, although they may have traveled abroad and returned to the United States prior to that date. One traveler fought at the side of the Mujahidin against the Soviet forces occupying Afghanistan in the 1980s but was arrested in 2009 for plotting an attack on the United States. Others had joined al Qaeda or the Taliban in Afghanistan, al Shabaab in Somalia, AQAP in Yemen, or Jabhat al-Nusra or ISIS in Syria. Still others had traveled to obtain training from jihadist instructors in Pakistan.

Several of the more recent travelers were teenage girls who had been persuaded to come to Syria by the promise of romance or adventure. Although they are included in this analysis, U.S. authorities decided to treat them as runaways rather than would-be jihadists and thus returned them to their families instead of prosecuting them.

A Statistical Profile

This section offers a profile of the travelers, including the following:

- age at the time of travel or arrest for attempted travel
- gender
- citizenship status
- country of origin (of those born abroad)
- education level
- year of travel or arrest for attempted travel
- whether the person was born into or converted to Islam
- whether the person appears to have radicalized in the United States
- destination
- preferred jihadist group
- whether the person was intercepted before reaching his or her destination
- fate or status.

Some data about the individual travelers are invariably missing. For example, court documents often omit information about citizenship, such as how the foreign-born became citizens and when they entered the United States. Sometimes, but not always, these details can be gleaned from press accounts. But because information is missing, the figures in each category rarely add up to the total number of travelers in the data set (280). Where I compare subsets of travelers, the numbers get small very quickly. The reader should keep this mind when looking at some of the percentages. Reasonable confidence is warranted for the broad trends, but caution is in order where the conclusions are drawn from fewer cases.

Age at the Time of Travel or Arrest for Attempted Travel

The average age of the American travelers when they departed or were arrested for attempting to reach a jihadist front abroad was 25; the median was 24. (In this report, all reported *averages* are means; medians are also often reported.) Age information was not available for 19 of the 280 travelers in the data set.

Gender

Jihad is a predominantly male occupation. Of all travelers, 261 were men, and only 19 were women.

Citizenship Status

Some details regarding citizenship were available for 257 of the travelers. As shown in Figure 4.1, 136 are known to have been born in the United States. Available information suggests that another 13 were probably born in the United States. That would make native citizens account for 53 percent of the total when counting only those known to be born in the United States, or 58 percent when counting both.

Figure 4.1
Traveler Citizenship Status

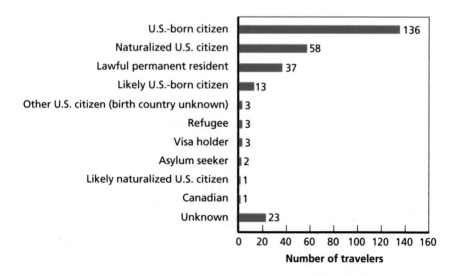

Another 58 people are known to have been naturalized U.S. citizens, and one other was most likely a naturalized citizen. For an additional three people who are known to have been U.S. citizens, it is not known whether they were born in the United States or were naturalized. Another 37 travelers were lawful permanent residents, three were refugees, two were asylum seekers, and three were in the United States on visas (some of whom had overstayed). One was a Canadian citizen who left the United States for Syria while on a visit to his father in Minnesota. As indicated previously, citizenship details for 23 individuals were not available.

Of the 257 travelers for whom information on citizenship was available, 248 (96 percent) were U.S.-born citizens; U.S. citizens of unknown birth country; naturalized citizens; or lawful permanent residents, who are usually long-term residents. The fact that so many were citizens or long-term residents suggests that, in the vast majority of cases, radicalization and recruitment took place in the United States. This is underscored by the age of the immigrants when they arrived in the United States (usually as children) and the age when they attempted to travel for jihadist purposes (an average of 11 years later).

Country of Origin
Of the 280 travelers in the data set, 116 are confirmed to have been born outside the United States (although their citizenship statuses are not always known). The country of birth is known for 112 of these travelers. The known 112 came to the United States from 37 countries, and just two of those countries account for more than 35 percent of the total number of foreign-born travelers. As shown in Figure 4.2, Somalia leads the list with 27 travelers, and 14 of the travelers were born in Pakistan. The numbers then drop off to five each for Iraq and Bangladesh; four each for Jordan, Syria, and Yemen; and three each for Afghanistan, Albania, Bosnia, India, Morocco, and Uzbekistan. The remaining countries have two or one each. Looking at the origins of the foreign-born travelers by region, 40 came from Africa (including the 27 from Somalia), 28 from the Middle East and North Africa, 22 from South Asia, eight from the Balkans, seven from Central Asia, five

Figure 4.2
Country of Origin of Foreign-Born U.S. Travelers

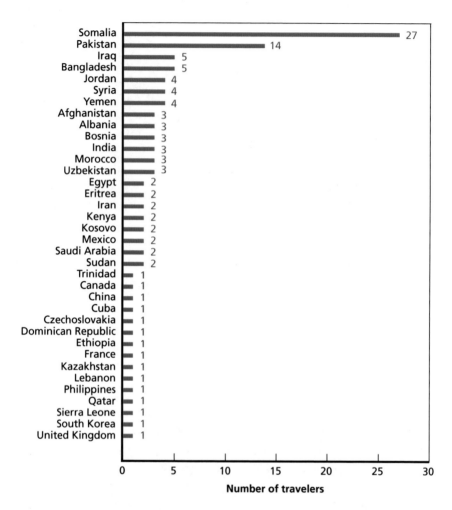

from Latin America, three each from the European Union and East and Southeast Asia, and one from Canada.

Country of origin appears to be a poor indicator of intention to join jihadists abroad. The preponderance of Somalis reflects the unique circumstances in Somalia and in one particular Somali community in the United States. These factors are discussed later in this section.

Education Level

Information about the highest level of education attained was available for 190 of the 280 travelers. As shown in Figure 4.3, 26 individuals had less than a high school degree, and 45 had obtained a high school degree. Two others were known to have attended high school, but whether they graduated was not known. A total of 117 of the travelers had attended at least some college. Of these, 21 had graduated with an undergraduate degree, and an additional 13 had gone on to postgraduate studies.

The percentage of high school dropouts among travelers (14 percent) is about in the middle of the U.S. national average reported during the period studied for this report (20 percent in 2000 and 10 percent in 2019). Travelers in the data set seem to have graduated from college at a lower rate (18 percent) than the average for Americans (24 percent in 2000 and 35 percent in 2019), but that may be due, in part, to the comparative youth of the traveler population.[3]

Figure 4.3
Traveler Education Level

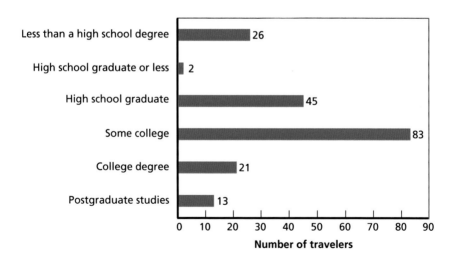

[3]   Kurt J. Bauman and Nikki L. Graf, *Educational Attainment: 2000*, Washington, D.C.: U.S. Census Bureau, Census 2000 Brief, August 2003; and U.S. Census Bureau, "Educational Attainment in the United States: 2019," webpage, March 30, 2020.

Year of Travel or Arrest for Attempted Travel

Table 4.1 shows the years that those in the data set traveled or attempted to travel. Information was available for all 280 travelers. There was an increase in travel and attempted travel starting in 2007, a drop back to some earlier levels in 2010 and 2011, and then a much greater increase starting in 2012. The peaks are explained later in this chapter.

Born into or Converted to Islam

Religious conversion can occur for various reasons, including marriage, spiritual searching, and personal crisis. Converts are often viewed as being more fervent in their beliefs than are those born into a religion. Of course, this is a generalization and is not meant to imply that converts are dangerous fanatics. However, research has shown that converts place greater importance on their religion than nonconverts do, believe in the tenets of their faith with greater certainty, and believe that theirs is the one true faith.[4]

The religious status of those who traveled to join jihadist fronts abroad may be significant in understanding the process of radicalization and recruitment. Of the 240 travelers for whom such information was available, 170 (71 percent) are known to have been born into the Muslim faith. Whether they were practicing Muslims is not known. At least 70 of those 240 (29 percent) were converts (see Figure 4.4). That percentage is above the national average for converts to Islam (23 percent).[5]

Travelers who were born into the Muslim faith were not necessarily pious or even practicing believers. Some were, but others have been described as not being very devout. For some, radicalization and recruitment to jihad were a form of rebirth—the adoption of a new identity.

---

[4]   Allison Pond and Greg Smith, "The 'Zeal of the Convert': Is It the Real Deal?" Pew Research Center, October 28, 2009.

[5]   Besheer Mohamed and Elizabeth Podrebarac Sciupac, "The Share of Americans Who Leave Islam Is Offset by Those Who Become Muslim," Pew Research Center, January 26, 2018. See also Pew Research Center, *America's Changing Religious Landscape*, Washington, D.C., May 12, 2015; and Williams, Chandler, and Robinson, 2018.

Table 4.1
Year of Travel or Arrest for Attempted Travel

Year	Number of Travelers
1989	1
1990	1
1998	3
1999	1
2000	8
2001	21
2002	4
2003	4
2004	5
2005	4
2006	6
2007	13
2008	17
2009	16
2010	9
2011	3
2012	18
2013	25
2014	53
2015	41
2016	9
2017	8
2018	1
Specific year unknown[a]	
Pre-2012	3
2012 or later	6

[a] There are nine individuals who traveled to Syria after the civil war there began in 2011, but the precise year of departure is unknown.

Figure 4.4
Travelers Who Were Born into the
Muslim Faith and Those Who Converted

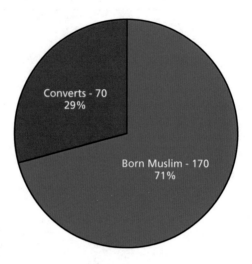

Converts - 70
29%

Born Muslim - 170
71%

Radicalized in the United States or Elsewhere

It was possible to ascertain the age at the time of entry into the United States for only 59 of the 116 travelers known to have been born abroad. Because I also know the age at the time of travel or arrest for attempted travel, I can ascertain how long these 59 people were in the United States before going or attempting to go abroad. Among these 59, the average age upon entry into the United States was 15; the median age was 14. The average number of years between their entry and travel or arrest was 11 years; the median was 10. These data suggest that most of the foreign-born travelers were radicalized after their arrival in the United States.

There were seven travelers who spent four years or less in the United States before attempting to travel to join jihadist organizations, and these seven had originally arrived in the United States when they were between 19 and 33 years old. It is difficult to say when or where these individuals were radicalized. Three of them were from Iraq and traveled or attempted to travel to Syria or Iraq. Another traveler, originally from Somalia, left the United States in 2000, just two years after arriving. He intended to join ethnic Somalis fighting in Ethiopia, but he was unable to find their camp. He then tried unsuccessfully to join an al-Ittihad al-Islami (a predecessor of al Shabaab) camp in neighboring Somalia before returning to the United States. He was arrested four years later in a plot to blow up a shopping mall in Ohio. Of these seven people, four were arrested before connecting with a jihadist group.

Destination

Information about all 280 travelers' intended destination countries was available; see Figure 4.5. (Note that many travelers were arrested before reaching their destinations.) Travelers generally headed to the sound of guns—in other words, conflict zones where there was a chance to get in on the fighting.

Syria attracted most of the American travelers, including those who went there to join the rebellion against the Assad regime; those who went there to live in the Islamic State proclaimed by ISIS in 2014, which covered territory in both Syria and Iraq; and those who were arrested in various countries on their way to the Islamic State. The exodus to Syria reflects the pull of Syria's civil war and the accessibility of the country from abroad. A flight to Istanbul and an easy run to the Turkish border brought travelers adjacent to their destination.

Somalia was the intended destination for the second-most travelers, followed by Afghanistan and Pakistan. Yemen was a distant fifth.

The significantly larger number of travelers going to Syria than to any other destination also reflects the excitement among Islamists worldwide that was caused by ISIS's creation of the caliphate in 2014. This development resulted in a component of travelers who wished to help build or simply live in what was advertised as an authentic Islamic society but who did not necessarily want to fight. Some of these individuals, however, may have been subsequently pressed into military service.

Finally, the large number traveling to Syria demonstrates ISIS's effective exploitation of the internet and social media in attracting recruits from abroad. Although some research has found that in-person contacts played a major role in recruiting and facilitating travel from the United States to Syria, it would be an overstatement to say that

Figure 4.5
Traveler Destination

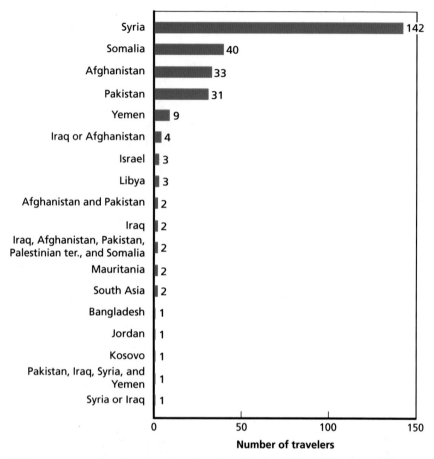

NOTE: In some cases, available information identified multiple destinations for a given traveler (e.g., *Afghanistan and Pakistan*). In other cases, a traveler intended to join a particular group abroad, but the exact country was not known (e.g., *Iraq or Afghanistan*).

there was an organized jihadist underground in the United States. However, there was a patchwork of jihadist connections, some reaching back to the Balkans conflicts in the early 1990s.[6]

[6] Meleagrou-Hitchens, Hughes, and Clifford, 2018.

Table 4.2 illustrates how destination preferences have changed over time. Getting to al Qaeda in the years before and immediately after 9/11 meant going to Afghanistan. Later travelers wanting to join al Qaeda headed to Pakistan. Pakistan replaced Afghanistan as the intended destination of choice in 2002, but the numbers of travelers to Pakistan also declined by 2004, and Syria later became the most popular intended destination.

The Somalia Experience Alerted U.S. Authorities

Between 2000 and February 2019, 40 U.S. residents traveled or attempted to travel to Somalia to support jihadist organizations (two others included Somalia among desirable destinations, but neither made it to any jihadist front). There was a sharp peak in the number of travelers to Somalia beginning in 2007. This reflected an increase in the number of Somali Americans returning to Somalia after Ethiopia, a historical enemy of the country, invaded in 2006. The increase also reflected the activities of a recruiting effort in a Somali American community in Minneapolis, Minnesota. Between 2005 and 2011, 28 U.S. residents went to Somalia, five others were arrested before leaving the United States, and one was arrested while en route.

Until the civil war in Syria, more Americans went to Somalia than to any other country. Almost all of them were from Minnesota, where there is a large community of recent Somali refugees with continuing close connections to their homeland. It is a troubled community, many of whose young men have had difficulty integrating into American society. Some of those who went to Somalia were members of street gangs, and some had criminal records.

Ethiopia's invasion of Somalia in 2006 aroused passions in the Minneapolis and other Somali émigré communities, where local sentiments were clearly on the side of those fighting the invaders, and the Somali diaspora mobilized to support the homeland. In addition to recruiting individuals to go to Somalia, some Somali Americans were involved in fundraising and other forms of support.

For the supporters who went to Somalia in 2007 and early 2008, nationalism, clan ties, and war stories told by veterans of Somalia's earlier conflicts appear to have been just as important motivators as jihadist ideology was—perhaps even more so. Nevertheless, jihadist ideol-

Table 4.2
Traveler Destination, by Year

Year and Destination	Number of Travelers
1989	
Afghanistan and Pakistan	1
1990	
Afghanistan and Pakistan	1
1998	
Afghanistan	1
Pakistan	2
1999	
Afghanistan	1
2000	
Afghanistan	3
Pakistan	4
Somalia	1
2001	
Afghanistan	14
Pakistan	7
2002	
Afghanistan	1
Pakistan	2
Yemen	1
2003	
Iraq	1
Pakistan	3
2004	
Iraq or Afghanistan	2
Pakistan, Iraq, Syria, and Yemen	1
Somalia	1
Yemen	1

Table 4.2—Continued

Year and Destination	Number of Travelers
2005	
Bangladesh	1
Iraq	1
Pakistan	1
Somalia	1
2006	
Afghanistan	2
Jordan	1
Somalia	3
2007	
Israel	3
Pakistan	2
Somalia	8
2008	
Afghanistan	2
Kosovo	1
Pakistan	2
Somalia	11
Yemen	1
2009	
Iraq, Afghanistan, Pakistan, Palestinian territories, and Somalia	2
Pakistan	6
Somalia	4
South Asia	2
Yemen	2
2010	
Afghanistan	1
Iraq or Afghanistan	2
Somalia	5
Yemen	1

Table 4.2—Continued

Year and Destination	Number of Travelers
2011	
Pakistan	1
Somalia	2
2012	
Afghanistan	5
Mauritania	2
Pakistan	1
Somalia	3
Syria	7
2013	
Afghanistan	1
Syria	21
Yemen	3
2014	
Somalia	1
Syria	52
2015	
Libya	1
Syria	40
2016	
Libya	2
Syria	6
Syria or Iraq	1
2017	
Afghanistan	1
Syria	7
2018	
Afghanistan	1
2012 or later (specific year unknown)	
Syria	9

ogy may have been the primary draw for some, certainly for the later volunteers and for those few who were not of Somali origin. It clearly motivated Omar Hammami, who traveled from Alabama to Somalia to become an effective spokesman for al Shabaab until he was killed, reportedly because of an internal dispute in the group.

Prior to the rise of ISIS in Syria, Somalia was also the only destination where there was a semblance of an organized recruiting effort and a pipeline for moving recruits. This system was eventually broken up when the recruiters were arrested. All of the travelers going to Somalia intended to fight, not to train for action elsewhere. This was evident in the fate of the 29 recruits who succeeded in getting there before 2012 (in addition to the previously mentioned 28 who made it to Somalia between 2005 and 2011, one more traveled there in 2000). By 2014, 15 of these individuals were known to have been killed, five of them in suicide bombings. Four of the 29 returned to the United States, where they were eventually arrested; three others were arrested abroad.

Once it became apparent that young Somali Americans from Minnesota were turning up in Somalia, U.S. and local authorities alerted Somali communities across the United States and worked with the Somali community in Minneapolis to halt recruiting. From 2010 to February 2019, only a handful of individuals traveled from the United States to Somalia—five in 2010, two in 2011, three in 2012, and one attempted in 2014. Since then, no one has attempted to travel there to support jihadist organizations.

Although al Qaeda encouraged al Shabaab to attack the United States and although the United States has carried out military operations against al Shabaab's leaders, the group remains focused on its local struggle. It has extended its operations beyond Somalia's borders only to neighboring Uganda and Kenya. Those two nations deployed troops as part of the African Union Mission in Somalia, which has assisted the Somali government in its conflict with al Shabaab.

The fact that Americans in Minnesota were being recruited for terrorist activities made it clear to U.S. authorities that organized recruiting operations for jihadist fronts abroad could be carried out in the United States. The Somali experience also alerted the authorities that they needed to focus attention on intercepting these would-be jihadists before they departed the United States. As noted earlier, once the authorities realized the scale of what was going on, they enlisted the cooperation of the Somali community in Minnesota and Somali immigrants in other parts of the country to halt jihadist recruiting. The response is now seen as a case study in countering violent extremism.

Most Traveler Destinations Were Not Original Homelands

The Somali Americans were a special case, but most of the American travelers were not going back to the countries of their birth. Only eight of the at least 145 travelers who headed to Syria or Iraq were originally from one of these countries, and only nine of the 36 travelers who went to Pakistan were born there. None of the travelers heading to Yemen was born there. Only one of the dozens of travelers to Afghanistan was Afghani. In contrast, 20 of the 42 travelers going to Somalia were born in Somalia, and almost all of the rest were of Somali ancestry. The diversity of travelers' nationalities overall and the diversity of travelers to each jihadist front underscore the observation that travelers adopted the Islamist claim of a single community of Islam—the *umma*—which commands the loyalty of all Muslims.

Preferred Jihadist Group

Destination countries generally reflect the travelers' jihadist-group preferences (Figure 4.6). For example, those heading to Afghanistan sought to join al Qaeda or the Taliban. Those aiming for Somalia prior to 2008 sought to join the Islamic Courts Union or al-Ittihad al-Islami, predecessors of al Shabaab; those going to Somalia in 2008 or later ended up in al Shabaab. Those going to Yemen wanted to join AQAP. Those heading for Pakistan were generally interested in eventually linking up with al Qaeda or the Taliban, but some sought to join Lashkar-e-Taiba or other Pakistan-based groups.

The situation in Syria was more complicated. Most of the travelers going to Syria wanted to join ISIS or live in the Islamic State, but some wanted to join al Qaeda's affiliate, Jabhat al-Nusra. All but one of the travelers who wanted to join Jabhat al-Nusra left or intended to travel in 2014 or earlier. Besides that one person (who was arrested before his departure in 2015), ISIS attracted all of the Syria-bound

Figure 4.6
Travelers' Preferred Jihadist Group

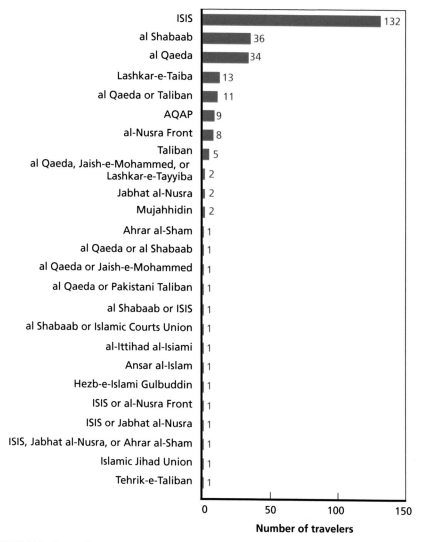

NOTE: This figure distinguishes between Jabhat al-Nusra and al-Nusra Front, although, in many cases, these are the same organization. The version used reflects the organization identified in the source material for each case. Since the research for this report was completed, the group's name changed to Hayat Tahrir al-Sham.

travelers after its rapid expansion across Syria and Iraq and its declaration of an Islamic State in 2014.

Trying to identify travelers' preferred jihadist groups in Syria was further complicated by the shifting sands and fluid loyalties among the rebel formations. A traveler might join a group that would change its allegiance or be absorbed by another group. At the same time, group preference was not always important. Several of the travelers going to Syria indicated that they would join either Jabhat al-Nusra or ISIS. This reinforces an observation that I made about those involved in plotting jihadist terrorist attacks in the United States: Although the plotters might have claimed allegiance to al Qaeda or ISIS, the choice between the two seemed to be secondary to carrying out an attack. Action counted more than affiliation.

Interceptions of Travelers

Of the 280 travelers in the data set, 81 were arrested by U.S. authorities before their departure from the United States. Another 34 were arrested by foreign authorities, often in their destination country.

Of the 196 who were able to travel (there is no related information for three of the travelers), 158 made it to their destinations. Of these, 15 were unable to connect with a jihadist group, and 72 were arrested on the way back to the United States or soon after their return.

Traveler Fate or Status

The database was current as of February 2019, and by that time, 47 of the 280 travelers had been killed abroad, one died of a drug overdose after returning to the United States, and one died during an attack in the United States (he was also a plotter). Another 141 were serving prison sentences in the United States or were in jail awaiting sentencing (one more was in prison abroad). In the database, individuals are categorized as "still in prison" based on the original sentences imposed; however, a few were within months of their release date. Depending on sentence reductions, which are smaller in federal convictions, some travelers might already have been eligible for release by the time this report was published. Another three were serving prison sentences in Pakistan.

In addition, 38 travelers had served their sentences, some of which were reduced in return for cooperation, and had been released; two were subsequently deported to Qatar and Somalia. None of those who were freed after serving their sentences was known to have engaged in further terrorist plotting. Four female travelers, of whom three were teenagers, and one man were not charged and remained free in the United States.

Of the 40 travelers thought to have still been at large, 30 were reported to have gone to Syria and nine to Somalia; one might still have been in Afghanistan. Given the continued fighting and chaotic conditions in these three countries, some of these individuals are probably dead.

The fates of the 277 travelers for whom information was available are summarized in Figure 4.7. At the time of writing, 52 percent of them were in prison, and 2 percent were never criminally charged. An additional 14 percent had been sent to prison, completed their sentences, and had been released. Another 17 percent were reportedly killed abroad; two died in the United States: one of a drug overdose

Figure 4.7
Traveler Fate or Status

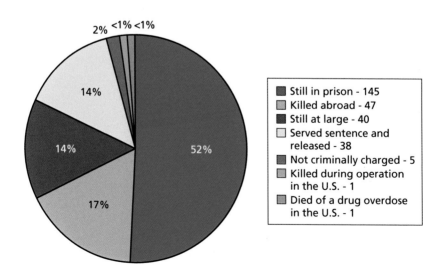

Still in prison - 145
Killed abroad - 47
Still at large - 40
Served sentence and released - 38
Not criminally charged - 5
Killed during operation in the U.S. - 1
Died of a drug overdose in the U.S. - 1

and one while carrying out a terrorist attack. As many as 14 percent of the travelers remained at large, although it is likely that some of these had also been killed.

An Exodus of Mavericks

In this study, the objects of analysis are not material items but rather human beings, and their lives do not fit neatly into the categories created by analysts. All such studies must deal with anomalies. Where the samples are large, a small number of peculiarities make little difference. But here, the missing and ambiguous data suggest that the assembly being examined contains a large proportion of mavericks—people who depart from a normal trajectory, make momentous life-changing decisions, and take extraordinary chances.

As noted earlier, few of the travelers in the data set were going to their country of birth or returning to an ancestral homeland. Most were going to countries they had never seen—conflict zones—not to visit but to fight, perhaps to die, or to obtain skills that would enable them to come back to the United States and carry out attacks that were likely to end in their own deaths or long imprisonment.

It can be argued that these decisions reflected the sincerity and intensity of these individuals' belief that there are no separate nations—only the House of Islam. The announcement of a caliphate provided a physical territory for the House of Islam to exist. In Islam, God will reward those who emigrate, and those who join jihadist fronts are breaking man's law, not God's law. The believers have a personal duty to defend the *umma*, the community of believers. Their lives rest in God's hands. Submission to this belief induces a kind of fatalism. Religious fanaticism can, of course, appear to secular observers as irrational behavior. True believers are out on the edge of any behavioral distribution curve. But, with the exodus of travelers to the Islamic State, the motivation appears to be more than belief.

To begin with, the travelers were self-selectors. Despite the proselytization campaigns and online appeals to emigrate, the exodus was only loosely organized. Rather than signing up through an organized pipeline, the travelers interacted with personal contacts who reinforced decisions and could assist travel. In some cases, these contacts were travelers themselves who communicated via the internet. (This phenomenon to personally handle things online may be similar to the way people today are more inclined to directly arrange their own travel rather than rely on travel agents.)

The recruiting process to deliver Pakistani and Arab fighters to Afghanistan in the 1980s was more organized, and the process to deliver volunteers to Syria from the surrounding Arab countries during the civil war there was perhaps more systematic; however, traveling from the United States was always a shambolic process. Many American travelers got on airplanes to fly to distant countries without knowing the local language and while having only the vaguest notion of how they might locate and join a jihadist group. Some had specific group preferences, but others did not. They sought merely to join the cause.

The lack of concrete planning is remarkable. The nonchalance displayed by the travelers may reflect their youth, lack of experience, or blind devotion to a cause. Many were in their late teens or twenties, and the barriers to relocation are lower for younger people, but not all of the travelers were young. Perhaps some of America's jihadists were just poor decisionmakers who embraced ideologies that allowed them to evade making difficult choices.

Hijrah (or migration) requires disassociation from the society of disbelievers. The individual biographies of the travelers suggest that many of them were already disassociated; they were unattached, alienated, dissatisfied, frustrated, bored, floundering, or all of these. Many sought solutions in converting to Islam or in rediscovering an extreme form of the religion of their birth. Already adrift, they found it easy to relocate. With the discounting of their own life situations, the risks were acceptable. Much seems to have been determined by individual circumstances, including what was going on in their lives at that moment and the people they happened to meet. The same seems to be true of those involved in carrying out or plotting to carry out terrorist attacks in the United States.[7]

---

[7] Jenkins, 2017.

These statements are my suspicions and speculations, not statistical findings. With all of the concern about homegrown terrorists and travelers seeking to join jihadist organizations abroad and with all of the efforts to counter violent extremism, there has been remarkably little behavioral research on the individuals who seek this path. This is true despite the scores of jihadist plotters and travelers who are in prison and who, theoretically, could be interviewed.[8] It is unlikely that psychological tests will reveal a jihadist or terrorist indicator, but such studies might better inform public policy.

Given the nonconformist, sometimes careless nature of the travelers' decisions to go abroad, it is not surprising that some of them became disillusioned with their situations and returned or sought to return to the United States. ISIS attempted to prevent such returns by taking away the passports of arriving volunteers. Captured ISIS documents also reveal the existence of shirkers, or individuals who tried to avoid hard combat duty by claiming illness or injuries or even volunteering to go back to their homeland as terrorist operatives.[9] Reports of executions in the Islamic State also reveal that desertions were a problem.[10]

---

[8] For two path-breaking studies involving interviews with jihadist travelers, see International Center for the Study of Violent Extremism, "About Breaking the ISIS Brand," webpage, undated; and Meleagrou-Hitchens, Hughes, and Clifford, 2018.

[9] Loveday Morris and Mustafa Salim, "A File on Islamic State's 'Problem' Foreign Fighters Shows Some Are Refusing to Fight," *Washington Post*, February 7, 2017.

[10] "ISIS Publicly Beheads Its Fighters for Desertion: Report," NDTV, January 31, 2016.

CHAPTER FIVE

Comparing Those Who Traveled Before 2012 with Those Who Traveled in 2012 or Later

In this chapter, I compare the travelers who went or attempted to go abroad before 2012 with those who did so between January 1, 2012, and February 2019. The dividing line, which reflects the pull exerted by the escalating Syrian civil war and the rise of ISIS, represents a shift in patterns. The broad conclusions from this analysis are highlighted in bold.

There was a higher volume in later years. A total of 116 U.S. residents were publicly identified as having traveled or attempted to travel from the United States to a jihadist group abroad between 1989 and the end of 2011. The earliest known traveler, Daniel Patrick Boyd, traveled in 1989 to join Hezb-e Islami Gulbuddin, a jihadist group then fighting Soviet forces in Afghanistan. In 2009, Boyd and seven other men—including his sons—were arrested for plotting jihadist attacks in the United States.

A total of 164 U.S. residents were identified as having traveled or attempted to travel to jihadist fronts abroad between January 2012 and February 2019. This is double the volume of the earlier period in a shorter time frame. The peak years were 2014 to 2016.

There was little age difference between the groups. The average age of those who traveled or attempted to travel to join jihadist fronts abroad prior to 2012 was 25; the median age was 24. The average age of those traveling in 2012 or later was 25; the median age was 23.

Given ISIS's extensive use of social media, one might have expected the organization to have reached an even younger audience, and it did indeed attract many teenagers. However, this was offset by the apparent appeal of the Islamic State to a greater number of older travelers.

More women traveled in later years. Armed jihad is male-dominated, but the later travelers included more women than the earlier group did. Of the 19 female travelers in the data set, only two went abroad prior to 2012; the other 16 traveled in 2012 or later. The two who traveled earlier—the only women who aimed to join al Qaeda—spoke about plans of eventually getting paramilitary training in South Asia, but they traveled initially to join other jihadists in Europe. One additional woman, in her thirties, is believed to have joined the al-Nusra Front in Syria. She was killed in a confrontation with government forces in 2013.

Other women joined or sought to join ISIS. Three teenage girls traveled to join ISIS families in Syria. Four were brought to the Islamic State by jihadist husbands, and one was brought to Syria as a child by her jihadist father.

More travelers in later years were converts to Islam. Of the 112 travelers before 2012 about whom such information was available, 82 (73 percent) were born Muslim and 30 (27 percent) were converts. By comparison, of the 128 later travelers for whom such information was available, 88 (69 percent) were born Muslim and 40 (31 percent) were converts. (Keep in mind that, because of missing information, these percentages may not reflect the percentages for all 280 travelers.)

Syria was the dominant destination of the later travelers. Prior to 2012, at least 36 travelers headed to Somalia and at least 30 went to Pakistan. During the earlier period, more than half of the intended destinations were in South Asia.

Of the 164 individuals who traveled in 2012 or later, 143 headed for Syria or Iraq. Eight intended to go to Afghanistan, and one headed to Pakistan. Yemen was the destination of three travelers. A total of 127 of the 143 later travelers sought to join ISIS, and three said that they intended to join either ISIS or Jabhat al-Nusra. Four people heading to other countries (Libya, Mauritania, or Somalia) indicated ISIS as their preferred group.

There was a sharp decline in al Qaeda's recruiting appeal after 2011. Only 15 of the later travelers sought to join the group or one of its affiliates, including al Shabaab, AQAP, and Jabhat al-Nusra. Had there been a competitor to ISIS, Jabhat al-Nusra might have gained additional recruits, but only eight travelers went or wanted to go to Afghanistan. The civil war in Syria propelled jihadist recruiting. When not counting travelers seeking to join or support the jihadist fronts that emerged during the civil war in Syria, jihadist recruiting dropped to 21 individuals over the nearly seven-year period (2012–2018). And the number of jihadists in the data set who headed to Syria after 2015 dropped to 14.[1] This suggests that military operations against al Qaeda and the Taliban in Afghanistan and against ISIS in the Middle East have made these destinations far less attractive. Somalia has also become a less-frequented destination for Americans seeking to support jihadist organizations.

Many more later travelers were intercepted before departure. Information on interception was available for all 116 pre-2012 travelers. Only 14 (12 percent) of them were arrested before leaving the United States. Two of the 14 who were intercepted attempted to leave before 2001, when authorities started watching more closely for travel to jihadist fronts abroad. Between 2001 and 2011, 81 travelers successfully left the United States, and 12 of the 14 interceptions came during this period.

For those who traveled in 2012 or later, the figures differ significantly. Interception information is available for 161 of the 164 travelers in this later group. Of these, 67 (42 percent) were arrested before leaving the United States. Percentages of interceptions of travelers in both periods are shown in Figure 5.1. The likely reasons that the percentages differ so much is because the Somali experience alerted U.S. authorities to the phenomenon of recruiting in the United States, and awareness of the intense online effort by ISIS to recruit foreigners to come to Syria helped authorities focus attention on preventing travel to jihadist fronts.

Traveler fate or status. By February 2019, 25 of the 116 pre-2012 travelers were reportedly dead, 49 were in prison in the United States,

---

[1]   In addition, nine individuals traveled to Syria after 2011, but the precise year is unknown. Of these, one was arrested in 2013, and three had been killed by 2015.

Figure 5.1
Interceptions Among Pre-2012 Travelers and Those Traveling in 2012 or Later

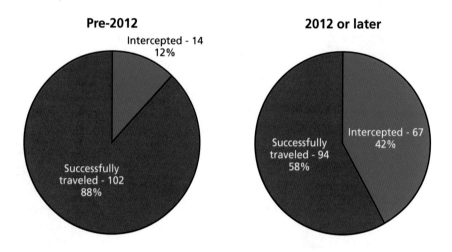

three were reportedly in prison abroad, 31 had served their sentences and been released, and eight were believed to still be at large.

Of the 164 people traveling in 2012 or later, 24 were reportedly dead, 93 were in prison, five were never charged with a crime, seven had completed their prison sentences and been released, and 32 were believed to still be at large. The fate of three was unknown.

A higher percentage of the later travelers were still in prison, which is not surprising because far fewer had completed their sentences. A much lower percentage were reported to be dead, leaving a higher percentage at large, although that could simply reflect a lack of information. Many of the travelers simply fell off the radar in Syria.

CHAPTER SIX

Comparing Homegrown Plotters with Travelers

Is there a discernible difference between the collective profile of U.S. residents who plotted to carry out attacks in the United States and that of people who went overseas to join jihadists? The plotters made a decision to directly attack the United States. In contrast, the travelers decided to leave the United States to fight for or otherwise assist jihadists in their armed struggle or to live in a society created by the jihadists. This would seem to be a different kind of a commitment and a different set of targets. In this chapter, I attempt to compare the profiles of these two groups.

The comparison presents a methodological challenge: Should the travelers who were also involved in subsequent terrorist plots in the United States be grouped with the plotters or the travelers? Fifty-four of the 280 U.S. residents who traveled or attempted to travel abroad were involved in subsequent terrorist plots in the United States; one individual who had been intercepted before departure and then released ended up participating in a subsequent terrorist attack. It would have been a mistake to eliminate these 54 travelers from a discussion of homegrown terrorist plots, so they were included in the earlier study of jihadists who carried out or plotted attacks in the United States.[1] These same 54 individuals were also included in the present analysis of travelers. However, they cannot be double-counted in the comparison of the two groups, so I have omitted them from the comparison and instead analyzed them as a separate third group.

---

[1] Jenkins, 2017.

Of the 196 people who plotted an attack in the United States between 9/11 and November 2019, 142 (72 percent) had not traveled or sought to travel abroad; of the 280 travelers examined in this study, 226 (81 percent) were not connected with any terrorist plot in the United States. In the next section, I compare the profiles of the plotters who did not travel and the travelers who did not plot or participate in an attack on the United States. In the section that follows that, I analyze the group of 54 individuals who were both plotters and travelers. In Chapter Eight, I examine the combined group of 422 American jihadists.

Plotters Versus Travelers

Gender. Travelers included a higher percentage of women. Only five of the nontraveling terrorist plotters (4 percent) were women. One of the five was arrested for lying to the Federal Bureau of Investigation (FBI) to protect her husband and does not appear to have been part of the plot, and another was part of the husband-and-wife team that killed 14 people in an attack in San Bernardino, California. In contrast, 18 of the nonplotting travelers (8 percent) were women. All but two were headed for Syria, although seven of them were intercepted before they got there, and several of the remaining women had been taken along as family members of male travelers.

Age. For nontraveling plotters, the average age at the time of attack or arrest was 30; the median was 27.5. The nonplotting travelers were, on average, younger. The average age for this group was 25; the median was 24. This could reflect the fact that the decision to leave the country is often easier, and perhaps more impulsive, for younger people.

Country of origin. Information was available for 141 of the 142 plotters who were not also travelers: Of these, 70 (50 percent) were born in the United States; 71 (50 percent) were born abroad. Pakistan was the birthplace of the most plotters (11), followed by Afghanistan, Bangladesh, and Somalia (four each). Of the 211 nonplotting travelers for whom information was available, 121 (57 percent) were born in the

United States; 90 (43 percent) were born abroad. Somalia had the most foreign-born travelers (24).

Time spent in the United States by foreign-born plotters and travelers. The age upon arrival in the United States was known for 52 of the 71 foreign-born plotters. Their average age upon entry was 15.5; the median was 16. These same 52 spent an average of 13 years in the United States before carrying out an attack or being arrested; the median was 12 years.

The age upon arrival was known for 41 of the 90 foreign-born travelers. The average was 15; the median was 14. The foreign-born travelers spent an average of 11 years in the United States before traveling or attempting to travel abroad; the median was also 11. The difference from the time plotters spent in the United States before attacking or being arrested was not statistically significant.

That the foreign-born travelers, on average, arrived in the United States at roughly the same age as the foreign-born plotters and spent roughly the same number of years in the United States before taking some kind of action or being arrested would seem odd, given that the plotters, on average, were five years older than the travelers. However, the age difference is explained by the fact that the U.S.-born plotters were, on average, four years older than the U.S.-born travelers.

Converts to Islam. Information about how religious affiliation occurred was available for 118 of the 142 nontraveling plotters: 61 (52 percent) were born Muslim, and 57 (48 percent) were converts. Information available on 186 of the 226 nonplotting travelers indicates that 132 (71 percent) were born into Islam, and 54 (29 percent) were converts. As these numbers indicate, the plotters were significantly more likely to be converts than the travelers were.

Those Who Were Both Travelers and Plotters

The comparisons in the previous section exclude the 54 U.S. residents who had both traveled or attempted to travel to a jihadist front and who were involved in a terrorist attack or plot in the United States. The statistical profile of these 54 people does not differ markedly from the profile of those who only traveled or plotted to carry out attacks in the United States.

All but one of the 54 individuals in this group were men. About half (28) of them were born in the United States, and about half (26) were born abroad. Their average and median age at the time of travel was 23. Their average and median age at time of arrest for plotting was 26. Information on age at the time of entry into the United States was available for only 17 of the 26 foreign-born travelers and plotters. Their average and median age upon entry was 15. They spent an average of 11 years in the United States between entry and travel or attempted travel. Sixteen of the 54 people (30 percent) were converts to Islam.

Traveling to join jihadist fronts abroad and plotting terrorist attacks in the United States combine in a variety of ways. Some of the travelers and plotters aspired to join jihadist groups overseas but, after seeing others being arrested, decided to participate instead in plots to carry out terrorist attacks at home. Others reached a foreign destination but were unable to link up with a jihadist group and came back to plot terrorist attacks in the United States. Several made multiple attempts to join terrorist groups overseas. Still others saw joining a jihadist front abroad as the culmination of a sequence of events beginning with attacks in the United States.

But of greatest interest to U.S. authorities are the 28 people who traveled abroad, managed to join a jihadist group, and then returned to plot attacks in the United States. They constitute 10 percent of all travelers and 14 percent of all plotters. These 28 were primarily members of an earlier cohort of travelers who joined al Qaeda or Lashkar-e-Taiba in Afghanistan or Pakistan and then returned to the United States, where they subsequently participated in terrorist plots. In some cases, it appears that the travelers went abroad with the purpose of acquiring training that would enable them to carry out attacks upon their return. In other cases, the travelers intended to fight abroad but volunteered or were recruited to instead return to the United States and carry out attacks. In still other cases, individuals who had joined jihadist groups abroad before 9/11 returned to the United States and years later became involved in terrorist plots.

Several people who aspired to join ISIS in Syria also participated in subsequent plots. Of those who actually joined ISIS and returned to the United States, none participated in any terrorist plot in the United States, because almost all of these individuals were arrested upon their return.

Only one returning jihadist veteran was able to attempt a terrorist attack. Faisal Shahzad, a naturalized citizen born in Pakistan, left the United States and received terrorist training from the Tarik-e-Taliban group in Pakistan. He then returned to the United States to build an incendiary device, which he attempted to detonate in New York City's Times Square in 2010. The bomb did not work, and he was soon arrested while trying to flee the country. Three other returning veterans (Najibullah Zazi, Zarein Ahmedzay, and Adis Medunjanin) also received explosives training in Pakistan, and Zazi, the group's leader, reportedly built the explosive devices intended for a suicide attack on New York City's subways. The plot was intercepted by U.S. authorities.

CHAPTER SEVEN

The Threat Posed by Returning Travelers

The travelers who are possibly still at large pose a threat to U.S. homeland security. Those who joined the ranks of al Qaeda, ISIS, and similar groups would be a particular concern. However, for al Qaeda to recover its role as the vanguard of the jihadist movement following the destruction of the Islamic State, it would need a spectacular attack that would restore its reputation and ability to draw recruits. Its ability to inspire homegrown terrorists in the United States was never great and now appears diminished. Al Qaeda has always preferred centrally directed attacks that rely on operatives infiltrated into the target country. AQAP twice came close to downing U.S.-bound aircraft. Recruiting operatives from foreign countries may offer further opportunities, although the recruits are more likely to be new volunteers who are not already on terrorist watch lists as returning travelers.

The destruction of the Islamic State, largely brought about by a U.S.-led bombing campaign and a ground offensive by U.S.-supported Kurdish and Arab fighters, gives ISIS (as an organization) and surviving ISIS veterans ample reason to want revenge. ISIS generally has not attempted the kind of strategic attacks favored by al Qaeda. Instead, it pursued a continuing propaganda campaign aimed at inspiring low-level violence. The campaign intensified as ISIS suffered significant losses of territory in Iraq and Syria. As a result of its efforts, ISIS was able to inspire several terrorist plots and successful attacks in Europe, fewer in the United States. The terrorist campaign in Europe reached a peak between 2015 and 2017.

Some analysts point to the deadly series of ISIS-assisted attacks in France and Belgium that occurred between 2014 and 2016 as evidence of a potential threat to the United States. However, a closer examination of that campaign suggests that circumstances are very different in the United States. In particular, the ISIS campaign in France and Belgium was coordinated by Abdelhamid Abaaoud, a Belgian national of Moroccan origin who went to Syria to join the fight against Assad in 2014 and used that country as a base for recruiting other Francophone fighters. Those fighters then infiltrated back into Europe, where they reconnected with local confederates who provided hideouts, transportation, logistics, and other pre-operational support, as well as additional volunteers.[1]

The success of Abaaoud's terrorist campaign depended on the exploitation of the massive flows of refugees from the Middle East into Europe, the absence of border controls inside Europe, and the lack of preparedness in and weak cooperation among the European states. Many of those who joined Abaaoud's campaign were already alienated young men who transcended the criminal underworld and radicalized underground that are deeply embedded in marginalized immigrant communities.

Galvanized into action, the European states have significantly improved the situation, and many subsequent terrorist plots have been thwarted, although the police and security services are still overwhelmed by the large volume of suspected homegrown extremists and returning fighters. According to Europol, the 2017 and 2018 attacks in Europe were mostly committed by lone individuals who had not been to a conflict zone but who may have been inspired by terrorist propaganda or the extremist narrative, as well as by other successful attacks worldwide.[2]

---

[1] Brian Michael Jenkins and Jean-François Clair, *Trains, Concert Halls, Airports, and Restaurants—All Soft Targets: What the Terrorist Campaign in France and Belgium Tells Us About the Future of Jihadist Terrorism in Europe*, San Jose, Calif.: Mineta Transportation Institute, 2016.

[2] Europol, *TE-SAT: European Union Terrorism Situation and Trend Report*, The Hague, 2018.

The same circumstances do not exist in the United States, where there is very little community support for people who wish to participate in or support jihadist organizations, the number of individuals requiring surveillance is much smaller, and there appears to be less of a radicalized underground. A one-off massacre with one or two perpetrators is always possible, as demonstrated by (1) the 2015 attack on a nightclub in Orlando, Florida, by a self-proclaimed (and apparently troubled) member of ISIS, in which 49 people died, and (2) the 2017 mass shooting in Las Vegas, Nevada, which has so far not surfaced any connections with extremist ideologies, in which 58 people were killed.[3] However, a sustained campaign of attacks in the United States does not appear likely.

Initial Intentions of the Travelers

Most of the travelers examined in this study went abroad to join jihadist organizations with the intention of fighting for their causes. The conflict in Syria also attracted some *jihadi tourists*—travelers who crossed the border into Syria just long enough to take and send home selfies and gain bragging rights but who stayed well away from the fighting. A few travelers went abroad with the initial intention of providing nonmilitary assistance, but some of these subsequently became fighters. A small number went merely to live among co-religionists and help build the caliphate announced by the leader of ISIS in 2014, and some were taken along as family members. Finally, several travelers went abroad to obtain the training and gain the technical expertise needed for terrorist operations that they already contemplated in the United States.

---

[3] I include the reference to the Las Vegas shooter not to imply that he has any nexus with jihadist ideology but merely to point out examples in the United States of the carnage that can be caused by a single individual.

High Attrition

To reach a foreign country, travelers had to avoid arrest in the United States or interception on the way. They then had to connect with a group abroad. Their destinations were all conflict zones, and some were killed in combat or volunteered for suicide missions. If they wanted to return to the United States, they had to avoid detection on the return route and arrest upon arrival. If they succeeded in not being caught upon re-entering the United States, they then could lie low or begin plotting attacks.

Journeys to foreign countries to engage with jihadist organizations have become more perilous since 9/11. For example, those traveling abroad prior to 9/11 were not subject to surveillance. The 9/11 attacks put authorities on guard, and entries were more closely monitored, but it was still possible to leave the country without arousing suspicion. As mentioned previously, that changed when U.S. authorities discovered the organized recruiting efforts among Somali Americans in the United States, and scrutiny of foreign travel intensified in response to ISIS appeals for foreign volunteers. Interceptions of would-be travelers increased dramatically starting in 2012.

Returning Travelers Who Become Plotters

Returning travelers who may be determined to launch terrorist attacks in the United States are the population of greatest concern to U.S. authorities, but, as the data in this report illustrate, that population is thus far small. Only 28 of the 280 documented travelers made it to their foreign destination, connected with a jihadist group, and returned to participate in or plot terrorist attacks in the United States. Of course, these numbers reflect individuals who were detected and arrested. It is not known whether others may have connected with jihadist groups abroad and managed to slip back into the United States unnoticed.

Only one individual, Faisal Shahzad, is known to have traveled abroad specifically to connect with a jihadist group, returned to the

United States, and attempted an attack.[4] He aroused some suspicion upon his return to the country but was not placed under surveillance, and local police where he lived were not notified of his presence.

Two deadly terrorist attacks were carried out in the United States by individuals whose time spent abroad may have contributed to their continuing radicalization, but they are not known to have connected with any terrorist group or received any terrorist training while overseas. Carlos Bledsoe spent time in Yemen and then returned to the United States, where he later opened fire on an Army recruiting office in Little Rock, Arkansas, killing one soldier and wounding another. After his arrest, he claimed to have been an operative of al Qaeda, but this was dismissed as a boast intended to elevate his own importance. Tamerlan Tsarnaev spent time in Russia and returned to the United States to carry out the 2013 bombing of the Boston Marathon with his brother. Their two bombs killed three people and wounded 264. On the run, the brothers later also killed a police officer. Russian authorities had earlier alerted U.S. authorities to the presence of Tsarnaev, but there is no evidence that he received any terrorist training while in Russia. Thus, neither Bledsoe nor Tsarnaev is considered a traveler by the definition outlined in this report.

Najibullah Zazi, Zarein Ahmedzay, and Adis Medunjanin, who received terrorist training in Pakistan, generated the most developed of the jihadist terrorist plots intercepted by U.S. authorities. Another trio, Jose Padilla, Lyman Faris, and Ali Saleh Kahlah al-Marri, were convicted of being al Qaeda operatives who were selecting targets for a wave of terrorist attacks following 9/11. They did not get very far in their planning. Padilla was arrested upon his arrival in the United States; al-Marri was arrested soon after his return; and Faris was arrested later.

Daniel Patrick Boyd, who had fought in Afghanistan with the Mujahidin, was arrested in 2009 for plotting terrorist attacks in the United States, but the plots had not gone beyond reconnaissance. Seifullah Chapman and Christopher Paul, travelers who were arrested for subsequent plots, had traveled before 9/11.

---

[4]   For more on many of the plotters in this section, see Jenkins, 2017.

Only one of the 31 jihadist terrorist attacks in the United States since 9/11 involved an individual who had received terrorist training abroad (Faisal Shahzad). Twenty-seven other travelers who managed to connect with jihadist organizations abroad were also involved in foiled terrorist plots in the United States, but the sequence of their activities varies. Two individuals were involved in terrorist plots in the United States and then fled to join a group abroad (Adnan Shukrijumah and Jude Kenan Mohammad). Two more left the United States, connected with a jihadist group, and became involved in terrorist plots in the United States while they were still abroad (Mohammad Omar Aly Hassan and Ahmad Abousamra). The remaining 23 individuals traveled abroad, connected with a jihadist group, returned to the United States, and were subsequently arrested in foiled terrorist plots. All but one of these occurred before 2011. Only one traveler connected with a group abroad, returned to the United States after 2010, and plotted an attack (Abdirahman Mohamud).

In addition to those individuals, Mohamed Abdullahi Hassan— a U.S. lawful permanent resident of Somali origin who returned to Somalia in 2008 to join al Shabaab—was connected to at least one attack in the United States.[5] While in Somalia, he remained in touch with jihadists in the United States, urging them to carry out attacks, and he was considered to be the instigator of the May 2015 shooting attack on the Muhammad cartoon exhibit in Garland, Texas. Hassan reportedly was also in touch with Syed Rizwan Farook and Tashfeen Malik shortly before their December 2015 attack in San Bernardino, California. Hassan turned himself in to Somali authorities several days after the San Bernardino attack. Because his crimes occurred while he was abroad, Hassan is not truly a traveler who returned to the United States to carry out an attack.

---

[5] Another jihadist plotter, John T. Booker, a self-proclaimed fighter for ISIS, used the name Mohammed Abdullah Hassan. Booker was arrested in 2015 for plotting to detonate a vehicle bomb at the Fort Riley military base in Kansas. The original or most famous person named Mohammed Abdullah Hassan was a Somali religious leader and nationalist who in 1899 declared a holy war on the British and Italian colonial powers and their local allies. The Dervish rebellion lasted 20 years.

Of all 280 travelers documented in this analysis, 19 percent participated in plots (this is the 54 people who were both travelers and plotters), but not all of them had connected with a terrorist group. There were 84 individuals who both connected with a terrorist group (148) and were not killed or captured abroad (47 were killed and 17 were captured abroad after joining a group); of those 84, 28 (33 percent) were arrested for plots after their return to the United States. Of the 76 pre-2012 travelers who connected with a terrorist group, 27 (36 percent) returned to plot or carry out terrorist attacks. In contrast, of the 72 who traveled in 2012 or later and connected with a terrorist group, only one had returned and been identified as plotting a terrorist attack (as of February 2019).

At the time of this writing, about 40 identified travelers were possibly still at large, although some of them traveled as far back as 2001. Some of these individuals probably have been killed since their whereabouts were last known. Of the 164 people traveling in 2012 or later, 32 were believed to still be at large. Thus, if all of those still at large were able to reenter the United States undetected, there would be a few dozen potential plotters, which would seem to be a manageable number for authorities to investigate, especially when compared with Europe. As far as public information shows, only one of the returnees from Syria has been able to return to the United States undetected. He remained in the country (apparently unknown to authorities) only briefly before returning to Syria and killing himself in a suicide bombing. However, FBI and other government estimates of the number of American travelers are much higher than the 280 documented here. If those estimates are more accurate, then more potential plotters could return to the United States after receiving jihadist training. Thus, if any of these individuals try to return, there is ample cause for vigilance and prompt arrest on charges of providing material support to a terrorist organization.

At the same time, travelers who may return to the United States determined to carry out armed jihad face greater obstacles than their European counterparts do. As noted earlier, the volume of travelers from Europe exceeds that from the United States by an order of magnitude. Moreover, those returning to the United States cannot count on disappearing into sympathetic undergrounds. Intelligence operations have proved extremely effective at uncovering and thwarting terrorist plots. Returning American travelers who are not promptly apprehended might even arouse suspicion among other potential jihadists that are informants or provocateurs. Therefore, because returning travelers may suspect that they are under surveillance, they are likely to remain isolated, avoided by others, and reluctant to reach out to like-minded people.

About 30 percent of the approximately 5,000 European residents who traveled to Syria had already returned to Europe by 2018.[6] These returnees represent a major challenge for European authorities and an indirect threat to the United States. U.S. officials worry that, because they are citizens of European countries, European veterans of Syrian jihadist groups will be able to more easily obtain visas for travel to the United States and thus carry out terrorist attacks on the U.S. homeland. Jihadist veterans could come from other countries, as well.

As indicated in the earlier analysis of America's jihadists, the vetting process that was tightened after 9/11 appears to have been effective thus far in preventing the entry of such plotting terrorists.[7] Most of the foreign-born plotters entered the United States as children and arrived before 9/11. They radicalized in the United States. But the Syrian civil war has vastly increased the population of jihadist fighters, so heightened vigilance is sensible. Indeed, defending against potential terrorist attacks is a long-term problem. Some of the U.S.-born jihadists were arrested for plotting attacks nearly two decades after their initial travel. European jihadists have also shown a dedication to violence that lasts many years and is unaffected—perhaps even intensified—by periods in prison.

---

[6]   Europol, 2018.

[7]   Jenkins, 2017.

Frustrated Would-Be Travelers

The statistics suggest that individuals who fail in their attempts to travel abroad to train with or support jihadist organizations may be more likely to engage in violence in the United States than successful travelers are. This observation, however, comes with a caveat: Showing intentions to travel abroad to conflict zones may bring an individual to the attention of authorities, making him or her an obvious and logical subject of surveillance and a potential target for a sting operation. Furthermore, those who successfully travel abroad for jihadist purposes and then attempt to return to the United States can be immediately arrested for providing material assistance to a terrorist organization, thus depriving them of any opportunity to plot and carry out an attack. Thus, when presented with a ready opportunity to join the jihad locally, frustrated would-be travelers might easily advance to become terrorists.

In other words, the fact that there are more would-be travelers than successful travelers among those who subsequently plotted attacks is a reflection of the law and investigative techniques. It is not known how many unidentified people may have seriously considered travel abroad and then abandoned that objective in favor of plotting an attack in the United States. Nonetheless, evidence of someone considering travel abroad to a conflict zone is a warning sign for future terrorist activity at home.

CHAPTER EIGHT

Statistical Profile of the Combined Population of Travelers and Plotters

My 2017 analysis of those who carried out or plotted terrorist attacks in the United States offered a tentative statistical profile of one category of America's jihadists.[1] Adding the travelers examined in this report brings in another dimension and more than doubles the size of the data set, thus allowing a higher level of confidence in the combined profile of American jihadists. With this larger population, the basic findings of the earlier work hold up.

The figures and tables in this chapter help describe this combined group of 422 jihadists. My analysis of the plotters covered in the earlier analysis, 54 of whom had traveled or sought to travel to jihadist fronts, is not replicated here. However, the list of plotters has been updated with 18 additional names (see Appendix B).

Figure 8.1 shows the population of jihadists broken down by how many were travelers, plotters, and attackers, or some combination thereof. In the analysis in this report, attackers are a subgroup of plotters. That is, all 36 attackers identified in the figure are included among the 196 plotters. However, this chart distinguishes the people who not only plotted an attack in the United States but managed to carry one out. In all other figures, the attackers are grouped with the plotters.

Age at the time of travel or arrest. The average age of the group at the time of first travel or arrest for plotting, attacking, or attempting

---

[1] Jenkins, 2017.

Figure 8.1
Combined Population of Jihadist Travelers and Plotters

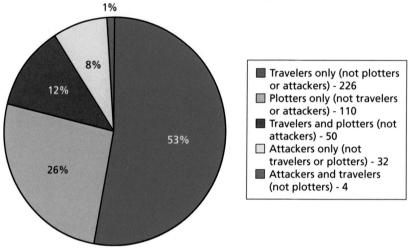

to travel was 27; the median was 25. In the earlier study, the 178 plotters had an average age of 29 and a median age of 27. The difference might be explained partly by the dates used for calculating age among the two groups: For plotters, I used the date of attack or arrest for plotting an attack; for travelers, I used the date that the individual first traveled abroad or was arrested for attempting to do so. Some of the plotters in the 2017 study had joined jihadist groups many years before participating in a plot, so it makes sense that they would be older at the time of attack or arrest. The travelers being somewhat younger affected the average and median ages of the combined group.

Gender. America's jihadists have been overwhelmingly male; there were only 24 women among the 422 plotters and travelers. The preponderance of men coincides with the earlier finding for plotters.

Citizenship status. Citizenship information was available for 394 of the 422 jihadists. More than half of the identified jihadists were born in the United States; 205 were verified to be U.S.-born, and available information suggests that another 14 were also born in the United States, accounting for 52 percent of the total jihadists in the data set and 56 percent of those about whom information was available. This is a somewhat higher percentage than that reported for the plotters in the earlier study (48 percent). An additional four people in the combined group were definitely U.S. citizens, but it was not possible to confirm whether they were U.S.-born or naturalized.

Of the 394 people for whom citizenship information was available, 171 were born outside the United States (including one person who was likely a naturalized U.S. citizen). Some of the 28 people in the unknown citizenship category, as well as the four people who were U.S. citizens with unknown birthplaces, may also have been foreign-born (see Figure 8.2). The large number of foreign-born jihadists might be a cause for concern: Are immigration vetting procedures failing? Does this number reflect assimilation issues? Of the foreign-born, 90 were reported to be naturalized U.S. citizens; one other was likely also a naturalized citizen. And 54 were lawful permanent residents. These citizenship statuses suggest that the jihadists spent a long time in the United States before arrest or travel. Only 12 of the foreign-born were in the United States on a temporary visa, and some of those visas had expired. Just four of the individuals entered the country illegally, so this is not a border security problem. The remain-

Figure 8.2
Citizenship Status, Travelers and Plotters Combined

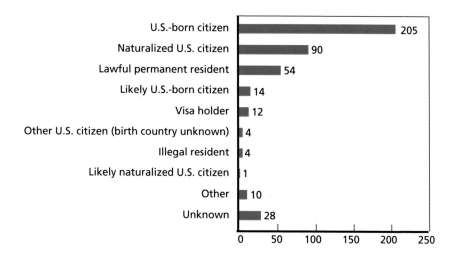

ing ten fall in the category of *other* (containing refugees, asylum seekers, and a Canadian citizen).

Number of years in the United States before travel or arrest. Of all 422 jihadists in the data set, 187 were foreign-born (citizenship status was known for 171 of these individuals). For 112 of those 187, information was available on how long the person had been in the United States before the qualifying event. Figure 8.3 shows the number of years that these individuals spent between arrival in the United States and either first attempt to travel or arrest for plotting, attacking, or attempting to travel abroad to join a jihadist group. The average was 12 years, and the median was 11. This finding is the same as the finding in the earlier analysis of plotters only.

Figure 8.3
Number of Years in the United States Before First Travel or Arrest for Plotting, Attacking, or Attempting to Travel Abroad, Travelers and Plotters Combined

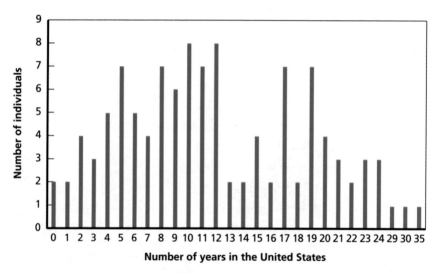

NOTE: No travelers or plotters were in the United States for between 25–28 or 31–34 years before the qualifying event, so those columns are excluded from this chart, for simplicity.

Country of origin. America's 187 foreign-born jihadists came from at least 48 countries. As shown in Table 8.1, Somalia leads the list with 31, followed by Pakistan with 25, Bangladesh with nine, and Afghanistan and Iraq with seven. Four countries (Albania, Jordan, Morocco, and Uzbekistan) account for six each. Muslim-majority countries dominate the list, but 14 of the jihadists (7 percent) came from Balkan countries (including Albania); 17 came from Latin American and Caribbean countries.

Table 8.1
Country of Origin, Foreign-Born Travelers and
Plotters Combined

Country of Origin	Number of Travelers and Plotters
Somalia	31
Pakistan	25
Bangladesh	9
Afghanistan	7
Iraq	7
Albania	6
Jordan	6
Morocco	6
Uzbekistan	6
Egypt (one unconfirmed)	5
Yemen	5
Bosnia	4
India	4
Kosovo	4
Saudi Arabia	4
Syria (one unconfirmed)	4
Cuba (one unconfirmed)	3
Eritrea	3
Ethiopia	3
Guyana	3
Iran	3

Table 8.1—Continued

Country of Origin	Number of Travelers and Plotters
Trinidad and Tobago (one unconfirmed)	3
Dominican Republic	2
Haiti	2
Kenya	2
Mexico	2
Sudan	2
United Kingdom	2
Algeria	1
Canada (unconfirmed)	1
China	1
Czechoslovakia	1
France	1
Ghana	1
Guinea	1
Honduras	1
Kazakhstan	1
Kuwait	1
Kyrgyzstan	1
Lebanon	1
Nicaragua	1
Palestinian territories	1
Philippines	1
Qatar	1
Russia	1
Sierra Leone	1
South Korea	1
Turkey	1
Unknown	4

Education level. Information on education level was available for 273 of the 422 jihadists. Of these, 41 dropped out of high school, and at least 66 completed high school or gained an equivalent degree. There is some uncertainty about whether three more completed high school. At least 113 attended some college, 31 more graduated with a four-year degree, and 19 had some postgraduate education (Figure 8.4).

Born into or converted to Islam. Information on whether the jihadists were born into the Muslim faith or converted was available for 358 of the 422 individuals. Of these 358, 231 (65 percent) were born Muslim, and 127 (35 percent) were converts. This figure is lower than but similar to the 38 percent reported in the earlier analysis.

Being Muslim by birth does not, by itself, indicate piety of faith and certainly not radicalization. The individual biographies of some of the jihadists instead point to a rediscovery of their birth religion and the adoption of a stricter form. At the same time, converting to Islam does not mean knowledge of the faith. In fact, several of the converts were described as having only a superficial knowledge of Islam and its precepts. And, in some cases, it was the attraction of jihadist violence that led the individual to adopt Islam.

Figure 8.4
Education Level, Travelers and Plotters Combined

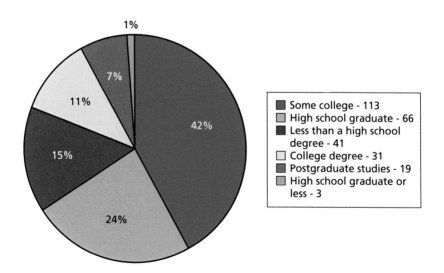

- Some college - 113
- High school graduate - 66
- Less than a high school degree - 41
- College degree - 31
- Postgraduate studies - 19
- High school graduate or less - 3

Year of first travel or arrest for plotting, attacking, or attempting to travel abroad. Figure 8.5 shows the number of individuals who first traveled or who were arrested for plotting, attacking, or attempting to travel, by year. The figure gives an idea of the volume of activity by time frame, but it is not precise. For example, some of earliest jihadists in the data set first went abroad prior to 9/11, and they were arrested years later in subsequent terrorist plots. And for the 54 people who were both travelers and plotters, it is possible that many years elapsed between the travel and the plot. Indeed, two of these individuals were arrested for plotting terrorist attacks 18 and 20 years after they left the United States to join jihadist fronts. In other cases, the plot and the intended departure may have been part of a single plan. In addition, there is surely some period of time between the date that an individual began plotting an attack and the date of arrest for such plotting; in some cases, plots unfolded for months, even years. Finally, some of the dates of arrest may not reflect an increase in terrorist activity but rather intensified law enforcement activity, as occurred immediately after 9/11, for example.

Figure 8.5
Year of First Travel or Arrest for Plotting, Attacking, or Attempting to Travel Abroad, Travelers and Plotters Combined

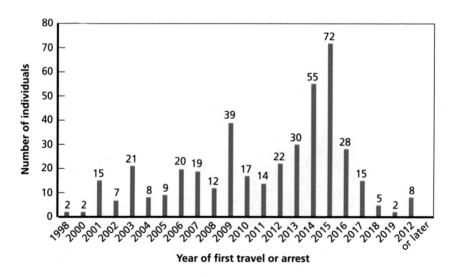

Having noted these caveats, I can identify some clear trends from the data in the figure. Decisions by individuals living in the United States to join the armed jihad increased after 9/11: The number of jihadist events (mostly plots) jumped sharply to 70 in the three-year period 2007–2009, fell back to 53 events in 2010–2012, and then again surged to 157 events (mainly attempts to travel) in 2013–2015. Travel attempts peaked in 2014—when ISIS swept across Iraq and announced the creation of the caliphate—then declined as ISIS began to come under increasing pressure; 2015 was the peak year for terrorist plots in the United States.

Since 2015, both the number of attempts to travel overseas and the number of plots to carry out attacks in the United States have declined: Only 49 events occurred between 2016 and February 2019 (the cutoff date for collecting traveler events for this report); two additional plotters were arrested in April 2019. ISIS had lost its luster. Other jihadist fronts in Afghanistan and Africa remain potential destinations for Americans seeking to join the fight, but there has been no call for foreign volunteers, and it is more difficult to reach these countries than it is to reach Syria.

Preferred jihadist group. The jihadist group preferences of the 363 American travelers and plotters for whom information was available reflect the trajectory of jihadist activity just described. Al Qaeda and its affiliates, along with other South Asia–based groups, dominated in the early years of this analysis, and ISIS dominated in later years. Al Shabaab had its own special constituency. At the same time, the prevalence of multiple choices, as shown in Table 8.2, suggests that the drive to action came first, and specific affiliation came second.

Table 8.2
Preferred Jihadist Group, Travelers and Plotters Combined

Group	Number of Plotters and Travelers
ISIS	174
al Qaeda	67
al Shabaab	35
Lashkar-e-Taiba	14
al Qaeda or Taliban	10
AQAP	8
al-Nusra Front	8
AQAP	5
Jaish-e-Mohammed	4
Jam'iyyat Ul-Islam Is-Saheeh	4
Taliban	4
al Qaeda or Jaish-e-Mohammed	2
al Qaeda or Lashkar-e-Taiba	2
ISIS or AQAP	2
Islamic Movement of Uzbekistan	2
Jabhat al-Nusra	2
Ahrar al-Sham	1
al-Ittihad al-Islami	1
al Qaeda or al Shabaab	1
al Qaeda or Hamas	1
al Qaeda or Jamaat al Muslimeen	1
al Qaeda or Pakistani Taliban	1
al Qaeda or Taliban	1
al Shabaab	1
al Shabaab or ISIS	1
al Shabaab or Islamic Courts Union	1
Ansar al-Islam	1
Hezb-e-Islami Gulbuddin	1
ISIS or al-Nusra Front	1
ISIS or Jabhat al-Nusra	1

Table 8.2—Continued

Group	Number of Plotters and Travelers
ISIS, Jabhat al-Nusra, or Ahrar al-Sham	1
Islamic Jihad Union	1
Jaish-e-Mohammed	1
Jaish-e-Mohammed or Ansar al Islam	1
Taliban (later ISIS)	1
Tehrik-e-Taliban	1

NOTE: This table distinguishes between Jabhat al-Nusra and al-Nusra Front, although, in many cases, these are the same organization. The version used reflects the organization identified in the source material for each case.

Fate or status. Information on the status of travelers and plotters, as of February 2019, was available for 407 of the 422 people in the data set. Fate has not been kind to them. As Figure 8.6 shows, 15 of the 36 jihadists who carried out attacks in the United States were killed during the operation or soon after. (One suspected plotter, Usaamah Abdullah Rahim, was killed in a confrontation with police who approached him for questioning.) All of the others were identified and arrested, many of them within hours. No one has gotten away from an attack, and there are no unsolved crimes. Almost all of the jihadist-inspired attacks carried out in the United States were single, isolated events.

Federal authorities arrested many of the travelers before they left the United States, and others were arrested upon their return. As of February 2019, 248 (59 percent) of the American jihadists in this data set (travelers and plotters combined) were in prison in the United States. At least another five were in prison abroad. Forty-six were convicted, served their prison sentences, and have been released. In other words, 71 percent of those who tried to plot attacks in the United States or join jihadist fronts abroad were arrested, convicted, and sent to prison. Five people who traveled to Syria were not charged.

Figure 8.6
Fate or Status, Travelers and Plotters Combined

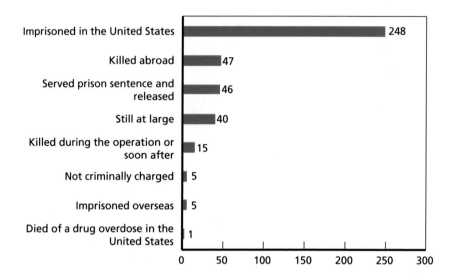

Of the 148 travelers who managed to join a jihadist group abroad, 47 (32 percent) were killed abroad, and one more died from a drug overdose after his return to the United States. An additional 40 (27 percent) remained at large; at least, there had been no report of their deaths. Because those individuals disappeared in war zones that have been the theaters of continuing conflict—some more than ten years ago—some of them had likely been killed.

CHAPTER NINE

Conclusions

The numbers in this report tell a story. They inform U.S. authorities and analysts about the dimensions and nature of the terrorist threat, the statistical profile of those who respond to jihadist recruiting appeals, the effectiveness of the U.S. response to the threat, and the results of that response.

The Threat

Those who plotted to carry out terrorist attacks in the United States and those who traveled or attempted to travel to join jihadist groups abroad represent two dimensions of the terrorist threat in the United States. Recruiting foreign volunteers strengthened the ranks of jihadist groups abroad and gave them a pool of potential operatives who could be sent back to targeted countries. As increased U.S. intelligence efforts and military operations abroad reduced al Qaeda's capabilities to launch large-scale terrorist attacks in the United States, inspiring homegrown terrorists became the primary way for the group to project power.

Although al Qaeda attracted thousands of foreign fighters to its camps in Afghanistan in the late 1990s, those fighters were mostly from outside the West and, to my knowledge, included very few Americans. After the U.S. invasion of Afghanistan in 2001, directing the remnants of resistance and organizing a new insurgency was a Taliban mission—al Qaeda's priority was to survive.

A small number of U.S. volunteers did show up in Pakistan or Afghanistan in the following years looking to connect with jihadist organizations. Some sought skills for terrorist operations that they wanted to carry out at home. Others went to fight, but then, because of boredom or a desire to elevate their own status, they proposed operations that they could carry out in the United States. These were potential operatives who required minimal investment by the jihadist groups. This low investment is reflected in the small number of travelers seeking to carry out terrorist plots upon their return and in the little success that those few travelers had.

The brief spurt of Somali Americans traveling to Somalia was a unique phenomenon, but it alerted U.S. authorities to the possibility of organizations recruiting jihadist fighters on American soil. It was not until the civil war in Syria that large numbers of foreign volunteers headed to that country. ISIS recruited fighters from all over the world as a source of manpower, and they eventually constituted a large share of the organization's fighting strength. The overall numbers of foreign fighters show this, although the U.S. contingent in ISIS remained small compared with those traveling from Europe and other regions.

Like al Qaeda, ISIS also exhorted its followers to launch attacks in their own countries, but it made little investment in operating overseas or in returning foreign volunteers as terrorist operatives. If ISIS wanted and was able to increase terrorist operations abroad after losing its territorial strongholds in 2019, American travelers who are theoretically still at large could provide a small reservoir of operatives. Revenge is a powerful motive, but that does not appear to be ISIS's strategy, and it is unclear that there is much of a reserve of American survivors still at large.

As of the time of this writing, travelers returning from Syria had not participated in terrorist plots in the United States; most of them had been arrested, convicted, and sent to prison. However, based on the biographies of individual travelers and plotters in the United States and in Europe, some of these individuals show persistence. In some cases, individuals decided to participate in jihadist plots years after traveling to jihadist fronts abroad. Some of those who were arrested spent years wavering between plotting and traveling. The jihadist narrative continues to have appeal, and individual actions remain a threat.

Statistical Profile of America's Jihadists

The Travelers

Of the 280 travelers examined in this report, 54 appeared in the previous analysis of 196 jihadist attackers and plotters,[1] so only 226 of the travelers are additions, bringing the total number of American jihadists in the data set to 422. The 280 individuals' travel extended over nearly 30 years, but when excluding a couple of early outliers, the period covered is closer to two decades. And more than half of the travelers left the United States after 2011, almost all of those heading to Syria and wanting to join ISIS. These findings suggest that Syria's civil war offered a unique confluence of appeal and accessibility. There are no similar flows to other less-accessible or less-inviting jihadist fronts.

The travelers themselves differ only marginally from the jihadists who plotted to carry out terrorist attacks in the United States. The travelers were, on average, younger, and a few more of them were women. More than half of them were born in the United States. The travelers born abroad, like their counterparts who were plotters, came from more than 30 countries. Most had arrived in the United States as children and spent roughly the same number of years there between their arrival and their attempt to join the jihad, which suggests that, as was the case with the plotters, most of them radicalized in the United States. Many more were U.S.-born converts to Islam. These findings suggest that America's jihadists do not reflect an immigration problem; that is, it does not appear that radicalized individuals are being admitted into the United States or that vetting is failing. America's jihadists are made in the United States.

Few travelers headed for hard-to-reach destinations or sought to join jihadist fronts that were under intense military pressure. Counterterrorist operations clearly reduced travel. As military campaigns in Iraq and Syria closed the ring on the Islamic State, foreign travel to that destination dropped off sharply.

---

[1] Jenkins, 2017.

Travelers and Plotters Combined

Combining the travelers with the plotters who were examined in the 2017 analysis more than doubled the population of American jihadists, but it did not result in any significant change in the jihadists' combined profile. This analysis therefore reinforces the results of the earlier research. Whether individuals sought to travel to jihadist fronts abroad or intended to participate in jihadist plots in the United States seems to reflect circumstances and opportunities rather than any difference in profile.

The increase in the number of jihadist travelers and plotters seen around 2014 and 2015 was due primarily to the allure of ISIS and the caliphate, and the number of travelers fell sharply with the organization's loss of territory. The fact that decisions both to travel and to plot involved individuals rather than larger groups indicates that jihadists have not been able to organize themselves in the United States' Muslim community. The large percentage of converts to Islam among the travelers and plotters underscores this observation. For instance, by definition, the converts come to Islam from outside the community. For many, there is little evidence of regular mosque attendance or relationships with members of the community, and they often display only superficial knowledge of the religion.[2]

The experiences of America's jihadists are in sharp contrast with the experiences of the terrorist groups that were active in the United States during the 1970s and early 1980s. Members of the earlier groups had sympathetic constituencies and were able to evade arrest and continue terrorist campaigns over many years. That is not the pattern of contemporary jihadist terrorism.

Although the more-recent travelers and plotters indicated preferences for particular jihadist groups, their choices did not reflect strong loyalties. They were looking for a connection anywhere they could find it, raising a banner to attract attention. The doctrinal disputes and organizational competition between al Qaeda and ISIS concerned them less. In most cases, their connection with either group was weak.

---

[2]   Aya Batrawy, Paisley Dodds, and Lori Hinnant, "Leaked Isis Documents Reveal Recruits Have Poor Grasp of Islamic Faith," *The Independent*, August 16, 2016.

Thus, it may be inferred that jihadist travelers and plotters are driven by internal motivations and circumstances as much as they are inspired by external groups and efforts.

The U.S. Response

After suffering the most deadly attack in the annals of terrorism on 9/11, the United States has aggressively pursued jihadist militants abroad and at home. The U.S. response has been tough and effective; some would describe it as relentless and unsparing. U.S.-led military campaigns in Afghanistan, Iraq, and Syria have dispersed al Qaeda and ended the territorial assertion known as the Islamic State. As of early 2020, U.S. armed forces were involved in military operations and military assistance programs in North and West Africa, the Philippines, the Arabian Gulf, and other locations around the world aimed at improving local capacity to deal with jihadist insurgents and terrorist campaigns.

Through these efforts, the operational capabilities of jihadists have been degraded. U.S. targets abroad, including inbound commercial airliners, are still at peril, but jihadist groups now depend primarily on exhortation of homegrown terrorists to carry out attacks in the United States. Jihadist leaders have been driven underground. Many of them, including the jihadists' most-influential communicators with Western audiences, have been killed. Jihadist communications continue, although the volume has declined.

Those who portray U.S. counterterrorism efforts as exclusively comprising military operations fail to recognize the intense U.S. intelligence effort—including domestic intelligence—and the robust law enforcement campaign against the jihadists. Given where U.S. authorities were and what the country faced after 2001, even allowing for an exaggerated sense of alarm in the immediate shadow of 9/11, that campaign can be judged a success.

Part of the success derives from the strength of U.S. society. There is little evidence that jihadist ideology has gained much traction among Muslim Americans. For instance, there are an estimated 3.45 million

Muslims residing in the United States, and I found that, between 9/11 and spring 2019, only 422 people were motivated by jihadist ideology to wage religious war by plotting to carry out terrorist attacks in the United States or traveling to join jihadist fronts abroad.[3] (During those same years, more than 4,000 Muslim Americans joined the U.S. armed forces, and many of them served in Afghanistan and Iraq.)

The significance of the number of American jihadists identified in this research depends on point of view. The existence of more than 400 lawbreakers, many of whom were violent or willing to support violence, clearly poses a danger in any society.

As part of the U.S. response, foreigners suspected of possible terrorist connections are being kept out of the United States. But most of the travelers and plotters were born in the United States or arrived as children. Only a few were in the United States on temporary visas. Still, scrutiny of visa applicants has increased.

Since 9/11, U.S. authorities uncovered and thwarted more than 80 percent of the domestic jihadist terrorist plots in the United States, and those suspected of terrorist intentions were identified and arrested.[4] Since 2011, most of the intended travelers were intercepted before leaving the United States or in transit. Those who reached their destinations and returned were arrested. There has been no need to suspend habeas corpus (which protects against unlawful imprisonment), detain suspects by executive order, or hold special tribunals. The courts have worked. The conviction rate has been extremely high, and the sentences have been severe.

These efforts have not prevented every attack, and total success would be an unreasonable expectation. Since 9/11, 36 people inspired by jihadist ideology have been able to carry out 31 terrorist attacks in the United States. These attacks killed 105 people, not counting the attackers, and one attack (in Orlando, Florida) resulted in 49 of those fatalities. That is a tragic toll, but spread over the time frame, it amounts to about six fatalities per year. Such terrorism was intended

---

[3] Others who offered jihadist groups various forms of assistance but did not participate in any terrorist plots will be discussed in a future report.

[4] Jenkins, 2017.

to create fear and alarm, as these attacks did. However, in a country that regularly suffers mass shootings and that, between 2001 and 2018, averaged 16,000 murders annually—amounting to more than 280,000 dead for the nearly 18-year period—six fatalities per year hardly constitutes a significant contribution to the continuing level of violence.[5]

Americans seeking to join the global jihad, either in the United States or abroad, should realize where it most likely leads. Of the jihadists (travelers and plotters) examined in this report, 70 percent had been sent to prison, and 60 percent remained there. At least half of those who slipped by U.S. authorities to join jihadist groups abroad had died. The attrition rate of approximately 90 percent is an undeniable success for U.S. authorities, yet it has come at a price of many lives taken in a few acts of terror.

Costs and Criticisms

Protecting U.S. homeland security, if military operations are included, has been a costly enterprise in blood and treasure. And it can be argued that the continuing presence of U.S. forces in Afghanistan, the U.S.-led invasion of Iraq in 2003, the U.S.-assisted overthrow of the government in Libya, the U.S.-led bombing campaign in Syria and Iraq, and U.S. support for the Saudi-led military campaign in Yemen have stoked hatred, given jihadist recruiters new wind, and produced a global jihadist movement with far more members than it had on 9/11.

But counting jihadists is tricky. Being affiliated with al Qaeda or pledging allegiance to ISIS has offered advantages to insurgents in the Middle East, Africa, and elsewhere. But affiliation does not mean that the insurgents take orders from a central jihadist command or that they should be counted as global jihadists. Most remain committed to local objectives, not global jihad. Nonetheless, their existence portends an enduring security challenge for the United States and beyond.

---

[5] Disaster Center, "United States Crime Rates, 1960–2018," webpage, undated.

There are understandable criticisms of the U.S. domestic effort as well. In particular, it is based on suppression rather than dissuasion. The numbers cited in this report reflect application of the law, not the effectiveness of efforts to counter the jihadist narrative or prevent radicalization. However, although authorities and analysts know precisely how many terrorist plotters and jihadist travelers are in jail, they do not know how many would-be jihadists changed their mind or were discouraged or deterred from plotting crimes or offering their services to foreign groups.

Critics assert that police are not "so much 'getting better at stopping' plots as getting better at finding (and facilitating) embryonic plots to stop—ones that, earlier, would likely have never led to much but that would not have been uncovered."[6] It is true that many of the thwarted plots in the United States were uncovered while they were still inchoate notions in the minds of individuals who, in some cases, appear to have possessed only limited capabilities.

For example, when authorities wanted to test the determination of a suspect, the strategy of inserting confidential informants and undercover police, without crossing the line of entrapment (a common assertion by defense lawyers, which the courts invariably rejected), inevitably helped the suspect think more concretely. And providing a suspect with the means to carry out an attack—often fake explosive devices—acted as a psychological accelerant, actualizing a theoretical attack beyond what the perpetrator would have achieved on his own. The use of these strategies should not constitute a legal defense; in such cases, the suspect vocalized intentions and demonstrated willingness to take action in furtherance of an attack. It is also true that, by advertising violent intentions and then readily joining what they believed to be a real terrorist organization, jihadists could have just as easily been recruited and exploited by real terrorist operatives. Furthermore, one cannot dismiss the danger posed by determined individuals operating on their own with limited means.

---

[6] John Mueller, "What Happened to the Islamic State Foreign Fighters That Had Returned to Europe?" *National Interest*, November 5, 2018.

My own view is that the term *lone wolf* both inflates the overall terrorist threat to the nation posed by individual operatives and glorifies them. That does not mean, however, that such individuals are incapable of large-scale attacks. For example, a single person with firearms murdered 49 people in an attack in Orlando, Florida, and another person drove his vehicle into cyclists and runners on a bike path in New York City, killing eight. But, although such attacks are occasionally spectacular, they make only a minuscule contribution to the overall number of homicides in the United States, as noted earlier. Nevertheless, terrorist attacks have greater societal impact and cause greater alarm than ordinary murders do, so preventing terrorist attacks assumes a greater role.

Deterrence is not easily quantified, but it is a positive result to make would-be jihadist warriors wary of getting together because they might fall prey to police stings. A public perception that no one is safe anywhere and that police are helpless stokes alarm, which can have insidious effects. It is therefore important to show the public that terrorist attacks can be prevented and that perpetrators can be brought to justice. That requires proactive policing, including intelligence-gathering and undercover operations.

Some critics of the current U.S. domestic counterterrorism effort argue that more attention must be paid to countering violent extremism than to putting terrorists in jail. Skeptics counter that this tiny fringe of fanatics may not be susceptible to the community programs envisioned. Moreover, counter-radicalization raises the specter of government-sponsored programs aimed at patrolling thought.

Also of understandable concern is the gradual growth of a security state manned by a vast security bureaucracy enforcing an expanding array of surveillance and control measures. Of course, emergency measures are often necessary, and they can be peeled back when the emergency ends. But in this seemingly endless war on terror, the measures have become permanent features of the political and legal landscape, gradually accumulating and potentially altering the nature of U.S. society.

On the other hand, the U.S. legal system has worked. Apart from two individuals who were arrested in the United States and held in military custody for years before they were turned over to the civilian courts,[7] the defendants associated with terrorism have been charged with crimes, have maintained their civil rights, and were brought to trial before a judge or a judge and jury who could independently assess the evidence and decide whether the person was guilty. Of those who were tried, almost all were convicted. However, I do not assert that justice is perfect. An often sensationalist news media and an atmosphere of fear promoted by official statements from Washington, threat-mongering politicians, and others with agendas beyond domestic security have fueled biases to which courtrooms may not always have been immune.

Despite all of its efforts, the United States will never succeed in eliminating the last jihadist, and it cannot claim that it has turned the corner or is on the verge of a strategic victory over the jihadist movement. The jihad launched by al Qaeda two decades ago will remain a part of the U.S. threat matrix for the foreseeable future.

---

[7]   Ali Saleh al-Marri, a legal resident of the United States, was arrested and held as an enemy combatant for more than eight years, and Jose Padilla, a U.S. citizen, was arrested in 2002 and held in military custody for more than three years.

Traveler Data Set

This study is based on data compiled on 280 U.S. persons (citizens and residents) who were publicly identified or arrested between 9/11 and February 2019 for traveling abroad or attempting to travel abroad to join a jihadist front (i.e., the travelers). The spreadsheet that contains the data on the 280 individuals is available online at www.rand.org/t/RR3195. The spreadsheet is a working document provided for reader convenience, and the data were current as of February 2019. Full citations are not provided, and some URLs might no longer be functioning. The spreadsheet text has not been edited.

As described earlier, the analysis in this report considers the 280 travelers, the 178 terrorist plotters included in the first analysis,[1] and 18 plotters added since the publication of that paper (see Appendix B of this report). And because 54 people were both travelers and plotters and should not be counted twice, the total number of individuals in the complete data set of America's jihadists is 422. There may be some names included on other chronologies of jihadist activity in the United States that are not found here, and there are a few names on this list that are not found on some of the other lists. No two lists entirely agree.

This list of 422 people includes only those who were publicly identified for or charged with assisting a specific terrorist plot or volunteering their services to jihadist fronts abroad; it does not include people who provided some other type of assistance, such as financial, materiel, or propaganda. Those individuals will be addressed in a future report.

---

[1] Jenkins, 2017.

Beyond the documented criminal cases examined as part of this research, there may be individuals who subscribed to jihadist extremist beliefs and were heading down the path toward criminal behavior but then dropped out because their life circumstances changed. These people do not identify themselves as almost terrorists; I (and authorities and other analysts) have no way of counting them. There also may be jihadist believers who were deterred from criminal action by their fear of apprehension. Although deterrence is a goal of law enforcement, I have no way to measure the number of potential plots or jihadist journeys that might have been deterred. Interventions by family and friends may have diverted others. In some cases, FBI agents or police officers simply talking to individuals whose actions or words aroused suspicion may have been sufficient to alter their behavior. I cannot quantify this gray area with any confidence or calibrate the presumed danger that would-be jihadists might have posed.

The remainder of this appendix focuses on the 280 travelers examined in this report. As noted earlier, *travelers* are defined in this report as U.S. persons—citizens, lawful permanent residents, long-term visa holders, and other residents of the United States—who traveled, attempted to travel, or intended to travel abroad to join jihadist organizations as fighters, support their activities in other ways, or obtain training that could be used in terrorist plots in the United States. Under U.S. law, it is a crime to provide material assistance to a foreign terrorist organization.

The list of 280 travelers (available in the spreadsheet provided as a supplement to this report) excludes foreigners who were recruited, equipped, and directed or who decided to come to the United States to carry out attacks. Examples of such individuals include the 9/11 hijackers, Richard Reid (who intended to detonate a device in his shoe), and Umar Abdulmutallab (who intended to detonate a device in his underwear).

I found information about the travelers in a variety of sources, including public announcements of arrests by the FBI and the U.S. Department of Justice, publications by the U.S. Department of Homeland Security, reports by the House of Representatives Homeland Security Committee, periodic publications and special bulletins issued by various fusion centers and local police departments, news media accounts, and reports published by other research centers.

Not all of the travelers were arrested in the United States; some were arrested and remain in prison abroad. Some were known from social media or other sources to have joined jihadist fronts but have since disappeared. Others were identified only after their deaths abroad. Some who were minors at the time of attempted travel have not been publicly identified.

Once I identified travelers for inclusion in this report, I acquired additional information from their criminal indictments, news media sources (often local reporters digging into the backgrounds of those arrested), reports of trial testimony, and media coverage of the trials. Names, places of residence, and ages were readily available, but citizenship status and date of entering the United States (if a naturalized citizen or lawful permanent resident) often remained stubbornly elusive. Sometimes, there was little information on the individual's education level. And it was sometimes impossible to determine whether an individual was born into the Muslim faith or was a convert, and, if the latter, how long the person had been a convert and what being Muslim meant to him or her. In some cases, conversion appeared to be little more than a superficial shift in self-identity.

In some cases, it was not possible to establish the date when the individual departed from the United States. And some individuals made more than one trip abroad in an attempt to join a jihadist group; or they managed to join one, come back to the United States, and leave again; or they were arrested on their second journey. For cases in which there were multiple trips, I used the date of the first departure for the analysis.

As described earlier in the report, U.S. Department of Justice and FBI officials estimated that between 250 to 300 Americans joined or tried to join ISIS in Syria and Iraq.[2] In my efforts for this report, I

---

[2] In 2015, U.S. Deputy Assistant Attorney John Carlin stated that 250 Americans went or tried to go overseas to join ISIS (Jonathan Dienst, "Number of Americans Trying to Join ISIS Doubles in a Year: Department of Justice," NBC New York, September 30, 2015). In 2017, a spokesperson for the FBI stated that 300 Americans "have traveled or attempted to travel to Syria and Iraq to participate in the conflict" (Hollie McKay, "Almost All American

was able to identify fewer than half that number, leaving many unaccounted for. Several explanations are possible. It could be that the U.S. government estimates were just that—estimates. Or it may not have been possible for us to precisely identify all of those believed to be U.S. persons. It is also possible that some of those who went abroad during the study time frame have not been publicly identified because they may still be under investigation or the subjects of sealed indictments. Some may have returned to the United States and become cooperating witnesses. Furthermore, the public estimate could include individuals who went to Syria to join other organizations (including the Kurdish Peshmerga or Free Syrian Army, which fought against ISIS), and, after investigation, authorities decided not to prosecute those people. Whatever the explanations for the difference in number, one should not assume that the list compiled for this report is complete.

Almost all of the 280 travelers in this analysis pleaded guilty or were convicted; legal proceedings continue for a few others. In five cases, prosecutors decided not to prosecute; for example, some were treated as runaways, and some accompanied their families as children. Those individuals are included in the analysis. However, anyone who was charged and found innocent was excluded from the list.

As mentioned earlier in the report, terrorist motives and mental health issues are sometimes hard to distinguish. In this analysis, I do not attempt to engage in remote psychoanalysis; instead, I follow the courts' decisions. Individuals found to be mentally incompetent to stand trial were excluded, and those undergoing court-ordered reviews of competency were held aside until there is a decision.

As in all research involving many individuals, there were some anomalies. For example, the United States has refused to repatriate Hoda Muthana (a young woman who joined ISIS in Syria) on grounds that, although she was born in New Jersey, her father was a foreign diplomat, and therefore she is not a U.S. citizen. That may be true from a legal perspective, but for the purposes of this research, I included her because, prior to traveling to Syria, she never lived anywhere but the

---

ISIS Fighters Are Unaccounted For," *New York Post*, October 27, 2017). See also Meleagrou-Hitchens, Hughes, and Clifford, 2018.

United States. Her inclusion is not meant to imply any opinion on the legal matter. In another case, Ali Saleh Kahlah al-Marri came to the United States to study, became a lawful permanent resident, returned to live abroad, and later joined a jihadist group, which led to his arrest. He is included among the 280 travelers.

Several of those who traveled to Syria claimed that they had not done so to join the jihadists but rather to offer humanitarian assistance or join the rebellion against the Assad regime and then, in the melee, ended up with jihadist formations. In other words, they were travelers but not jihadists. For example, Eric Harroun traveled to Syria to join the Free Syrian Army, but he claimed that he was captured by al Qaeda's affiliate Jabhat al-Nusra; he later saved the life of an injured al-Nusra fighter. Harroun was arrested after his return to the United States and charged with providing support to a foreign terrorist organization. He pleaded guilty to a lesser charge and was released. Months later, he died of a drug overdose.

Ahmed Farooq, despite being a U.S. citizen who later became a senior operative in al Qaeda, was excluded from the list of 280 travelers in the data set. Although Farooq was born in the United States while his father was in the country as a graduate student, the family returned to Pakistan when Farooq was still a very young child. He was thus technically a dual national but attended school in Pakistan. He joined al Qaeda in Pakistan in 2007 and rose to its upper ranks to become the organization's chief Urdu-language propagandist. He was killed by a U.S. drone strike in 2015. According to his mother, Farooq's U.S. citizenship was purely circumstantial. He was raised and educated in Pakistan and never mentioned his U.S. birth. Therefore, he was omitted from the list.

Despite a handful of these more-complicated situations, most of the cases were pretty straightforward. The individuals included in the data set traveled or sought to connect with a jihadist group abroad because they subscribed to the group's ideology and sympathized with its cause. Whatever their reasons, their actions violated U.S. criminal statutes.

My goal with this report was to provide a comprehensive group portrait of the American travelers, although, as noted, the list is surely incomplete. For instance, I do not know the total number of individuals who may have traveled to Afghanistan in the 1980s, to the Balkans in the 1990s, or to other conflict zones where jihadists were active. Furthermore, the information for the 280 travelers in the data set is sometimes incomplete. And, given the difficulties in obtaining some of the data, despite careful review, some errors are inevitable.

To view the spreadsheet of 280 travelers, which is a working file and has not been edited, visit www.rand.org/t/RR3195. That list is meant to align with Table 2 in the earlier analysis of plotters.[3]

---

[3] Jenkins, 2017.

Additional Plotters Since the 2017 Analysis

In the earlier work, *The Origins of America's Jihadists*, I analyzed 178 homegrown terrorists who, inspired by jihadist ideology, carried out attacks or plotted to carry out attacks in the United States between 9/11 and May 2017.[1] An epilogue to that paper called attention to three additional people who plotted or carried out attacks between June and October 2017 (Ftouhi, Solano, and Saipov). Solano and Saipov were included among the 422 people in this report's data set, but Ftouhi, who is not a U.S. person, was excluded.

Six more individuals were involved in terrorist attacks or plots between May 2017 (the cutoff date for the previous analysis) and April 2019 (the cutoff for adding plotters for this report) (Sayyed, Ullah, Jameson, El-Mofty, Azizi-Yarand, and Pitts).

It was also revealed in 2017 that U.S. authorities had been holding a Canadian national (El Bahnasawy) in custody since 2016 for planning terrorist attacks in the United States, and one U.S. person was connected with the same plot (Haroon). Because El Bahnasawy is not a U.S. person, he was not included as one of the plotters for this analysis.

Finally, after combing through various other sources, I identified an additional nine cases of plotters from as far back as 2006 (Haq, Clark, Barry, Farooqui, Abdirahman, Hassan, Johnson, Hamed, and Domingo). In this appendix, I note the reservations I have about including some of these individuals in the data set. At the end of this appendix, I identify five other potential plotters who were omitted.

---

[1] Jenkins, 2017.

Additions

On July 28, 2006, **Naveed Afzal Haq**, a 30-year-old U.S.-born citizen of Pakistani heritage, shot six women at the Jewish Federation in Seattle, one of whom died. During the attack, he said that he was motivated by hatred for the Jews, U.S. support for Israel, and the U.S. invasion of Iraq. Haq had a troubled history, was unable to hold a job, and had been arrested just months before the attack for exposing himself to passing women at a shopping mall. He reportedly had not attended a mosque for years, and a year before the attack, he had converted to Christianity and was baptized but then returned to his father's mosque just before his attack. He was diagnosed as suffering from bipolar disorder in 1996 and was taking powerful medication. At trial, his defense lawyer claimed that Haq was insane. The prosecution agreed that Haq was mentally ill but argued that he was legally sane at the time of the attack. Haq himself had objected to the insanity defense. His first trial ended in a mistrial. At his second trial, prosecutors introduced recordings of phone calls made by Haq while in jail in which he told his mother he was a "soldier of Islam." Washington state classified the attack as a hate crime; the prosecutor said that there was no evidence that the shooting was an act of terrorism. Haq had no reported contact with any foreign terrorist organization. Some, however, argued that Haq's manifest hatred reflected the ideology he shared with Islamic terrorist groups even though he was not a member of any group. The case raises the question of whether there is a meaningful distinction between a hate crime and a terrorist attack.[2] It also raises the question of what membership in a group means in the context of today's remote recruiting by exhortation. Does shared ideology suffice to consider someone a member?

Despite my reservations, I have decided to include this case, as well as several of the cases that follow, because to omit them would raise questions of author bias. Some of these individuals are described

---

[2]   "Seattle Shooting Suspect Grew Distant from Kin," NBC News, July 31, 2006; Jennifer Sullivan, "'You Should Be Proud,' Haq Told Mother After Shootings," *Seattle Times*, November 5, 2009; and Levi Pulkkinen, "Jewish Federation Killer Gets Life Without Parole Plus 120 Years," *Seattle PI*, January 13, 2010.

by government officials as jihadists. My general default decision is to include these, leaving the reader to make his or her own decisions.

On December 6, 2014, **Hudson Taylor Clark**, a 32-year-old U.S.-born Muslim convert, attempted to steal a handgun from a gun supply store in Cañon City, Colorado. When confronted by employees, he threatened them with a knife and left, but he was quickly located by a police officer responding to the call. In a scuffle during his arrest, Clark stabbed the officer, who then shot him. Clark survived and was charged with attempted murder. However, his trial was delayed for several years while Clark underwent a court-ordered psychiatric evaluation. Clark had previously claimed that Allah gave him a sign confirming that Clark himself was Jesus. Nevertheless, in 2018, he was ruled to be legally sane, found guilty, and sentenced to 14 years in prison. Although his commission of the crime is not in doubt, there is little publicly available information to indicate that this was a terrorist attack other than the fact that Clark reportedly made "Islamic-type statements" before and at the time of his arrest.[3]

On February 11, 2016, **Mohamed Barry**, a 30-year-old who emigrated from Guinea in 2000 and was in the United States on a green card, attacked diners with a machete at a restaurant in Columbus, Ohio. He wounded four and then escaped in his car. When he crashed in a subsequent car chase, he attacked police with the machete and was shot and killed. Although the FBI had looked at Barry for making Islamist threats four years earlier, that investigation had been abandoned. What motivated the 2016 attack is not clear, and federal authorities found no evidence linking him to any terrorist organization.[4]

On August 20, 2016, **Wasil Farooqui**, a 20-year-old U.S.-born citizen of Pakistani origin, injured two people in a stabbing attack at an apartment complex in Roanoke, Virginia. He claimed that voices

---

[3] "Suspect Accused of Stabbing Officer Showed Interest in Terrorism," KKTV News, December 9, 2014; and Sara Knuth, "Man Who Stabbed Cañon City Police Department Officer Sentenced," *Cañon City Daily Record*, April 15, 2019.

[4] Michael King, "Suspect in Restaurant Machete Attack Was on FBI's Radar," WCMH-TV, February 2016; Tim Stelloh, "'It Was Chaos': Victim Describes Brutal Machete Attack at Ohio Restaurant," NBC News, February 22, 2016; 10tv, "CBS Confirms Machete Attack Suspect Was in United States on Green Card," video clip, July 21, 2017.

had instructed him to carry out the attack. Farooqui had earlier come to the attention of the FBI when his parents notified authorities that their son was mentally ill and had traveled to Turkey, they feared, to join ISIS. Farooqui's mental state was brought up at his trial. He was described as having a schizoaffective disorder, which had been treated earlier. The court, however, did not accept that he was incompetent to stand trial. Farooqui pleaded guilty to malicious wounding and was sentenced to 16 years. At issue here, however, is whether this was a terrorist attack. Farooqui's prior travel to Turkey and his shouting of "Allahu Akbar" ("God is the greatest") at the time of the attack suggests jihadist inspiration, but federal authorities investigating the case said that they found no hard connection between Farooqui and ISIS. No terrorism charges were added to the original charge of assault. However, because he apparently traveled to Turkey in an attempt to join ISIS in Syria, he has been included in this analysis.[5]

On June 15, 2017, in Huntsville, Alabama, officers from the FBI's Joint Terrorism Task Force arrested **Aziz Ihab Sayyed**, a 22-year-old U.S.-born citizen who radicalized online, for planning to carry out bombings on behalf of ISIS. His targets included police stations and federal facilities in the state. Sayyed pleaded guilty and was sentenced to 15 years in prison.[6]

In October 2017, federal authorities revealed that they had secretly held in custody Abdulrahman El Bahnasawy, an 18-year-old Canadian citizen who had been arrested in the United States in May 2016. Two others were allegedly involved in El Bahnasawy's plot to carry out bombings targeting the subway, concert sites, and other sites in New

---

[5] Alicia Petska, "Roanoke County Stabbing Suspect Came Under FBI Investigation After 2016 Trip to Turkey," *Roanoke Times*, August 14, 2017; Matt Chittum, "Wasil Farat Farooqui to Serve 16 Years for Knife Attack That Drew National Attention," *Roanoke Times*, January 23, 2018; Elizabeth Tyree and Annie Andersen, "Man Connected to 'ISIS-Inspired' Knife Attack in Roanoke Co. Sentenced to 16 Years," WSET News, January 23, 2018; and "Update: Farooqui Sentenced to Serve 16 Years for Double Stabbing," WDBJ News, January 23, 2018.

[6] U.S. Department of Justice, "Alabama Man Sentenced to 15 Years in Prison for Attempting to Provide Material Support to ISIS," press release, June 20, 2018a; Jonece Starr Dunigan, "Citizen Tip Leads to Arrest of Man Facing Terrorism Charge in Huntsville," AL.com, March 6, 2019; and Ashley Remkus, "Alabama College Student Sentenced to 15 Years in Federal Prison for ISIS Bombing Plot," AL.com, March 7, 2019.

York City. **Talha Haroon**, a 19-year-old U.S. citizen, was arrested in Pakistan, and Russell Salic, a 37-year-old medical doctor, was arrested in the Philippines. El Bahnasawy was sentenced in December 2018 to 40 years in prison. Salic was ordered deported to the United States in mid-2018, and Pakistan has refused to extradite Haroon. (Because they are not U.S. persons, El Bahnasawy and Salic are not counted among the American plotters in this analysis.)[7]

On October 21, 2017, **Vicente Adolfo Solano**, a 53-year-old Miami, Florida, resident who had converted to Islam, activated the timer of what he believed was a bomb. It was instead an inert device that FBI agents, posing as members of ISIS, had provided to him. Solano, a Honduran citizen, had lived in the United States on temporary protected status since the late 1990s.[8]

On October 31, 2017, **Sayfullo Saipov**, a 29-year-old lawful permanent resident from Uzbekistan, drove a rented truck onto a bike path in New York City to run over cyclists and pedestrians, eventually crashing into a school bus. He killed eight people and injured 11. After crashing into the school bus, he exited his vehicle, shouting "Allahu Akbar" and brandishing two guns, which turned out to be a paintball gun and a pellet gun. Because neither was a lethal weapon, his actions may have been intended to deliberately draw police into shooting him. He was shot in the abdomen and arrested at the scene. He claimed that he committed the attack on behalf of ISIS. Saipov had entered the country in 2010, was married, and had three children. His attack appears to have inspired other vehicle-ramming attacks.[9]

---

[7] U.S. Department of Justice, "Charges Unsealed Against Three Men for Plotting to Carry Out Terrorist Attacks in New York City for ISIS in the Summer of 2016," press release, October 6, 2017; Manuel Mogato, "Philippines Doctor Linked to New York Attack Plot a 'Regular, Generous Guy,'" Reuters, October 10, 2017; and Stewart Bell, "Sentencing Delayed for Canadian Who Plotted ISIS Attack as Defence Prepares Medical Reports," *Global News*, February 13, 2018.

[8] "FBI: Florida Man Sympathized with Islamic State, Wanted to Bomb Mall," CBS News, October 23, 2017; Jon Herskovitz, "Honduras Man Living in Miami Charged with Trying to Bomb a Mall," Reuters, October 23, 2017; and Curt Anderson, "FBI: No Foreign Terror Links in Florida Mall Bomb Plot," Associated Press, October 26, 2017.

[9] Kim Barker, Joseph Goldstein, and Michael Schwirtz, "Finding a Rootless Life in U.S., Sayfullo Saipov Turned to Radicalism," *New York Times*, November 1, 2017; Nicole Chavez,

On November 12, 2017, **Mahad Abdirahman**, a 20-year-old Somali refugee, stabbed two men in a large shopping mall in Bloomington, Minnesota. At his trial, he claimed that he had been inspired by ISIS to carry out the attack. Abdirahman, who had a history of mental illness, had been treated the previous year for schizophrenia; he stabbed two staff members at the facility where he was being treated. However, a spokesperson for the Somali community in Minnesota stated that jihadist sentiments were widespread among Somali youth and that the U.S. government's efforts to prevent would-be jihadists from traveling abroad had unintended consequences locally.[10]

On December 11, 2017, **Akayed Ullah**, a 27-year-old lawful permanent resident from Bangladesh, detonated a bomb in the subway station connected to the Port Authority Bus Terminal in Manhattan. The attack was an apparent suicide bombing, but the bomb only partially detonated, injuring Ullah and five other people. Ullah arrived in the country in 2011 and, according to reports, began radicalizing in 2014 as a result of absorbing jihadist material on the internet. Ullah reportedly told police that he carried out the attack on behalf of ISIS, but he later claimed in court that he did not support the group; his motives remain unclear. He was angry at the U.S.-led campaign against ISIS, Israeli actions in Gaza, and President Donald Trump's recognition of Jerusalem as the capital of Israel. Convicted by a jury in November 2018, he faces a sentence of 30 years to life imprisonment.[11]

On December 20, 2017, the FBI arrested **Everitt Aaron Jameson**, a 26-year-old U.S.-born citizen and convert to Islam who had briefly joined the Marine Corps until he was discharged for failing to disclose

---

"What We Know About the New York Attack," CNN, November 1, 2017a; and "New York Truck Attack: Who Is Suspect Sayfullo Saipov?" BBC News, November 2, 2017.

[10] New America, "Terrorism in America After 9/11—Part II: Who Are the Terrorists?" Washington, D.C., undated; Tim Nelson, "Man Charged in Mall of America Stabbing Previously Committed to State Psychiatric Care," Minnesota Public Radio, November 15, 2017; Scott Johnson, "Minnesota Man Explains Mall Stabbings," *Power Line* blog, January 28, 2018; and Randy Furst, "Man Sentenced to 15 Years for ISIS-Inspired Knife Attack at Mall of America," *Star Tribune*, February 16, 2018.

[11] "Police Try to Trace Steps of Suspect in NYC Attack," CBS News, December 11, 2017; and "Port Authority Explosion: What We Know About Suspect Akayed Ullah," CBS News, December 11, 2017.

a history of asthma. Jameson was charged with plotting to carry out a Christmas Day attack at Pier 39, a popular tourist spot in San Francisco, California. Jameson told undercover agents that he planned to detonate bombs that would send people running into a killing zone where he could shoot them. The plot was aspirational; he had built no bombs and had no firearms. He was sentenced to 15 years in prison.[12]

On December 22, 2017, **Ahmed Aminamin El-Mofty**, a 51-year-old naturalized U.S. citizen from Egypt, opened fire on police officers at the state capitol building in Harrisburg, Pennsylvania, then fired at a responding police car, wounding the driver. El-Mofty was killed in a subsequent shootout with police. His motives remain unclear, and his inclusion here is open to debate. Although some agencies promptly labeled his actions a terrorist attack, investigating authorities found no evidence of radicalization. In addition, El-Mofty had been in a dispute with his ex-wife over custody of their children, which could suggest that personal motives were involved. This was possibly an incident of suicide by police.[13]

In January 2018, **Tnuza Jamal Hassan**, a 19-year-old student and the only woman among the 19 additional plotters, set a series of fires at St. Catherine's University in St. Paul, Minnesota. She also allegedly wanted to travel to Afghanistan to join al Qaeda. She was charged with arson and attempts to support foreign terrorists. Apparently, FBI officials had interviewed Hassan after becoming aware of her earlier intentions to travel to Afghanistan, but she was not charged at that time. The arson incidents occurred months later. Her trial, which was delayed by questions about her mental competency, was scheduled for early 2019 but was postponed again because of her mental health

---

[12] Justin Carissimo, "FBI: Man Planned ISIS-Inspired Christmas Day Terror Attack in San Francisco," CBS News, December 22, 2017; Ralph Ellis, "Terror Attack at San Francisco's Pier 39 Thwarted, Federal Authorities Say," CNN, December 23, 2017; Erin Tracy, "'Ready to Die': Modesto Man Suspect in Planned Christmas Attack in San Francisco," *Modesto Bee*, December 23, 2017; and Amy B Wang, "FBI Thwarts Alleged Plan to Carry Out Terrorist Attack in San Francisco on Christmas," *Washington Post*, December 23, 2017.

[13] Nicole Chavez, "Pennsylvania Police Shootings Were 'Terror Attack,' DHS Says," CNN, December 24, 2017b; and Mark Osborne and Ben Stein, "Pennsylvania Cop Shooting Suspect's 'A Chicken, Not a Terrorist': Ex-Brother-in-Law," ABC News, December 24, 2017.

issues. However, the court subsequently declared her to be competent to stand trial, so she is included in this analysis.[14]

On March 12, 2018, **Corey Johnson**, a 17-year-old U.S.-born citizen and convert to Islam, attended a sleepover at his friend's house, where he stabbed a 13-year-old boy, killing him; he also stabbed and wounded another teenager and that teen's mother. He claimed that he did so because they had offended his Muslim faith. The boys had been watching violent videos. Johnson was known to school authorities as a troubled, violent youth with white-supremacist, anti-Semitic, and anti-gay views who claimed to be an admirer of Adolf Hitler and Timothy McVeigh, the Oklahoma City bomber. He displayed a Nazi swastika on his Facebook page. It is not clear exactly when he adopted Islam or how devoted he was; authorities do know that he bought a Koran, a prayer cloth, and a Muslim skullcap. FBI agents met with Johnson in 2017 after they linked him to threats that had been made through social media to a Catholic high school in the United Kingdom. He was not arrested at the time, but findings from continued monitoring persuaded the FBI to seek an arrest warrant, which they were waiting for at the time of his attack. Given his identification with various extremist ideologies, Johnson seems to be another example of an attacker who blended multiple worldviews before committing violence and whose association with jihad is dubious.[15]

Although Johnson is included among the plotters in this analysis, the case raises several issues. For instance, the connection with jihadist-

---

[14] "St. Catherine Arson Spree Shows Difficulty in Predicting Terror Attacks," CBS Minnesota, February 17, 2018; Chao Xiong, "Former St. Catherine University Student Capable of Understanding Terrorism Charges, Doctor Testifies," *Star Tribune*, November 2, 2018; Sarah Horner, "Health Issues Delay Trial for Former Student Accused of Setting Fires at St. Catherine University," *Pioneer Press*, January 25, 2019; and Andy Mannix, "Psychologist: Suspect in St. Kate's Terror Case Now Competent to Face Charges," *Star Tribune*, December 20, 2019.

[15] Gary Detman, "Police: Teen Confesses to Stabbings, Converted to Islam," KCBY News, March 13, 2018; Steve Almasy and Chuck Johnston, "Florida Teen Held in Killing Was Being Investigated by FBI over Possible ISIS Interest," CNN, March 15, 2018; Eliot Kleinberg, "New: BallenIsles Killer Had Unsteady Family Life, from Missouri to Florida," *Palm Beach Post*, March 16, 2018; and Amy B Wang, "A Teen with Former Neo-Nazi Ties Claims His 'Muslim Faith' Led Him to Stab Three, Police Say," *Washington Post*, March 22, 2018.

inspired terrorism is tenuous. The attacker's beliefs were slippery; it is not even clear that Johnson should be called a Muslim, and the attack had no political objective. I included him in this analysis to illustrate the challenge in categorizing acts of terrorism. One should not automatically label just any act of violence by a Muslim to be terrorism. Is revenge for a perceived insult to one's beliefs an act of terrorism? Can a political agenda be assumed? Does watching a violent video beforehand by itself make an action terrorism? Must the perpetrator be of sound mind?

On May 2, 2018, authorities arrested **Matin Azizi-Yarand**, a 17-year-old U.S.-born high school student who, inspired by ISIS, planned to carry out a shooting attack at a suburban shopping mall near Dallas, Texas. He had been under investigation by the FBI since December 2017 and spoke with two informants and an undercover agent about his plans. Other targets included a school and a Hindu temple.[16]

On July 2, 2018, authorities arrested **Demetrius Nathaniel Pitts**, a 48-year-old U.S.-born citizen and radicalized convert to Islam, for planning an Independence Day attack in Cleveland, Ohio. Pitts, who had a record of felony arrests for assault, robbery, and theft, was on the FBI's radar since posting threatening messages on Facebook in 2015. He indicated to undercover agents that he wanted to join al Qaeda. He also talked about attacking St. John's Cathedral in Cleveland and attacking the children of military personnel.[17]

---

[16] Collin County (Tex.) Magistrate, affidavit for arrest warrant for Matin Azizi-Yarand, Warrant No. 18-136, April 30, 2018; Valerie Wigglesworth, "Plano Teen Arrested in ISIS-Inspired Plot to Commit Mass Shooting at Frisco's Stonebriar Mall," *Dallas Morning News*, May 2, 2018; and Stephen English, "'Fire Where You Hear Screams'—ISIS-Inspired Teen Allegedly Considered Other Targets," *Fort Worth Star-Telegram*, May 3, 2018.

[17] Jeff Mordock, "Ohio Man Accused of Plotting Terror Attack on Cleveland July 4th Parade," *Washington Times*, July 2, 2018; U.S. Department of Justice, "Ohio Man Arrested for Attempting to Assist a Foreign Terrorist Organization with Homeland Attack Plot," press release, July 2, 2018b; U.S. District Court for the Northern District of Ohio, criminal complaint against Demetrius Pitts, Case No. 1:18 MJ 2120, July 2, 2018; and Adam Ferrise and Eric Heisig, "Cleveland Terrorism Suspect's Penchant for Violence Stretches Nearly 30 Years," Cleveland.com, January 30, 2019.

On January 7, 2019, **Ismail Hamed**, an 18-year-old U.S.-born citizen, repeatedly called the Maricopa County Sheriff's Office in Fountain Hills, Arizona, asking to speak with a deputy. When a deputy sheriff went to see him in the parking lot, Hamed began throwing rocks at him and then brandished a knife. When he refused to drop the weapon, he was shot and wounded. He was charged with assault with a deadly weapon, but the charge was later amended to include terrorism under Arizona's statute.[18]

On April 26, 2019, FBI agents in California arrested **Mark Steven Domingo**, a 26-year-old U.S.-born citizen, for plotting to bomb a white-supremacist rally. Domingo was a former U.S. Army soldier who left the Army soon after serving a four-month tour in Afghanistan. He received a less-than-honorable discharge related to an incident there. Domingo described himself as a convert to Islam who wanted to seek revenge for the March 15, 2019, shooting at a mosque in Christchurch, New Zealand, but also contemplated attacks on Christians, Jews, and police officers. Domingo posted online that, to spur a civil war, the United States needed another event like the 2017 mass shooting at an outdoor concert in Las Vegas, Nevada. It was such online writings that brought him to the attention of authorities and led to an undercover operation. Domingo decided that he wanted to carry out a bombing like the 2013 attack at the Boston Marathon, and he sought assistance in building a pressure-cooker bomb. The Domingo case is interesting because it illustrates how previous events, such as the Boston bombing and the mass shootings in Las Vegas and Christchurch, can become reference points for subsequent plotters seeking to emulate or avenge such attacks. It also shows the fluidity of imagined targets.[19]

---

[18] "Islamic State Follower Seeks Lower Bond in Officer Assault Case," AZCentral.com, September 5, 2019; and BrieAnna J. Frank and Uriel J. Garcia, "18-Year-Old Shot by Deputy and Charged with Terrorism Released from Jail Prior to Trial," *Arizona Republic*, October 4, 2019.

[19] U.S. Department of Justice, "California Man Arrested in Terror Plot to Detonate Explosive Device Designed to Kill Innocents," press release, April 29, 2019; Richard Winton and James Queally, "L.A. Terror Plot Thwarted: Army Vet Planned 'Mass Casualties,' FBI Says," *Los Angeles Times*, April 29, 2019; and Richard Winton, "L.A. Suspect in Terror Plot Lived Quiet Life but Spewed Online Hate, Authorities Say," *Los Angeles Times*, April 30, 2019.

Omissions

The inclusion or omission of individuals in any compilation of jihadist terrorist attacks or plots can sometimes be controversial. At the heart of the matter is how one perceives and portrays the threat. Some tend to view Islam as the threat and thus view terrorism as simply one manifestation of an inherently aggressive belief system. Accordingly, under this perspective, all acts or threats of violence associated with Islam should be considered terrorism, regardless of whether they meet the definition of a terrorist crime. U.S. federal law defines *international terrorism* as "violent acts or acts dangerous to human life" that "appear to be intended to intimidate or coerce a civilian population; to influence the policy of a government by intimidation or coercion; or to affect the conduct of a government by mass destruction, assassination, or kidnapping."[20] If this collection of American jihadists strictly applied these criteria, however, I would have to exclude any terrorism-related activity other than that described in the federal terrorism statutes. I did not choose to be limited by that definition. In addition, prosecutions may take place at the state level, where definitions of terrorism vary. Inevitably, judgments are required in compiling a list of plotters and attackers.

Whether a case warrants being labeled as terrorism depends on the evidence of motive. In most terrorism cases, establishing motive is not a challenge because the actor proclaims his reasons for committing a violent crime. However, sometimes the motive or intention is a matter of interpretation (as it is in most criminal cases). Some of the cases discussed in this appendix lack clear evidence of motive, and a thoughtful prosecutor would hesitate to charge a defendant under a terrorism statute unless the motive element could be proved beyond a reasonable doubt at trial. Intelligence agencies and law enforcement organizations (as well as those outside of government who compile chronologies of terrorism) can be less concerned about motive; their task is to prevent terrorist attacks and apprehend perpetrators, who can be prosecuted for crimes other than the terrorism statutes (e.g., assault, homicide).

---

[20] U.S. Code, Title 18, Section 2331, Definitions, October 3, 2018.

U.S. law also makes a distinction between terrorism acts and *hate crime acts*, which are defined as "offenses involving actual or perceived race, color, religion, or national origin."[21] Attacks occurring as a consequence of anger at insults to Islam or hatred of Jews, absent ideological inspiration or political objectives, do not qualify as terrorism, but should one count religious beliefs as ideological inspiration?

Is shouting "Allahu Akbar"—which is a battle cry used by jihadists during attacks but is also a common Islamic expression used in a variety of circumstances—proof of jihadist inspiration? What about disturbed individuals who make threats and adopt the language or symbols of jihadist ideology in order to provoke police into killing them (often known as *suicide by police*)? Should they be considered terrorists?

Furthermore, must a person be of sound mind to be labeled a terrorist? Many people view all terrorism as illogical, insane behavior, but can terrorists be insane and still be considered terrorists? The U.S. legal system demands that a defendant be mentally competent, and a defendant can be found not guilty by reason of insanity. (A related question is whether researchers should identify, in a public document, individuals who have been found not guilty of terrorism-related charges.) Being found competent to stand trial, however, does not necessarily demand that terrorists or any other violent criminals be of "sound mind"—that is, capable of reason. Many violent crimes arise from disturbed states of mind, including personality disorders and extreme emotional distress. Again, answers to these questions are matters of judgment, so differences of opinion arise.

Whether all terrorist acts by Muslims should be labeled jihadist is yet another issue. U.S. government lists of jihadist acts include attacks, plots, and instances of material assistance that are inspired, enabled, or directed by foreign terrorists, but, in the age of the internet, what exactly are the criteria for an act to be inspired? Does the fact that an individual once looked at a jihadist video or read about a jihadist terrorist attack suffice? What if the perpetrator seeks to falsely blame an attack on jihadist terrorists in order to mislead the authorities? Gener-

---

[21] U.S. Code, Title 18, Section 249, Hate Crime Acts, October 28, 2009.

ally, I have tried to be inclusive in this analysis, partly to avoid accusations that I omitted some cases in order to deflate the jihadist threat. There are, however, five cases that I set aside and did not include for now, pending further information.

On August 18, 2012, 20-year-old U.S person **Nomad Khan** rammed his car into another car at high speed, injuring its occupants in Chicago, Illinois. When a security guard and later a police officer arrived at the scene to assist, he attacked them with a knife. During the ensuing scuffle, Khan said, "this is a war and jihad." He repeatedly demanded that the police officer shoot him in the head. He was shot in the hip and wounded and subsequently convicted of attempted murder and other charges. That Khan, who was not charged with terrorism, was guilty of attempted murder is not at issue. What gives pause here is whether there was any political motive behind Khan's actions or whether he was attempting suicide when he crashed his car or attacked police officers.[22]

On May 19, 2017, **Devon Arthurs**, an 18-year-old U.S.-born citizen living in Tampa, Florida, shot and killed two of his roommates because they disrespected his religion. He then took hostages at a nearby business before surrendering peacefully. Arthurs admitted to police that he murdered the two roommates, so his guilt in that crime is not in question. However, he told his hostages that he was upset about U.S. bombing in the Middle East. During the hours-long siege, he also told police officers that he and his roommates were neo-Nazis but that they had made fun of him when he converted to Islam. It is not clear how devout or serious Arthurs was about the conversion. He told police that his roommates were planning terrorist actions on behalf of their neo-Nazi group; the one surviving roommate admitted to those plans and was sentenced to 15 years in federal prison. Arthurs assisted authorities in the prosecution. What is at issue here is Arthurs' mental competence. He had a history of mental problems and was found by court-appointed psychiatrists to be incompetent to

---

[22] Circuit Court of Cook County (Ill.), appeal of the conviction of Nomad Khan, No. 1-15-0731, March 14, 2017.

stand trial. As of the time of this writing, he was being held at a state psychiatric facility.[23]

On June 21, 2017, **Amor M. Ftouhi**, a 49-year-old man with dual Tunisian and Canadian citizenship, stabbed a police officer at the airport in Flint, Michigan. Ftouhi reportedly shouted "Allahu Akbar" at the time of the attack. He also reportedly asked police after the attack why they did not kill him, suggesting a possible suicide motive. Ftouhi entered the United States only five days before the assault, so I did not consider him to be a U.S. person.[24]

Between January 24 and February 24, 2018, **Wesley Dallas Ayers**, a 27-year-old U.S.-born citizen, fabricated and placed three explosive devices and three hoax devices at various roadside locations in South Carolina. The devices contained notes indicating that ISIS was responsible and threatening to set off more-powerful devices in the future. One person was injured when he opened a basket containing one of the real devices. Ayers was subsequently identified, pleaded guilty in federal court, and was sentenced to 30 years in prison. At first glance, the incident appears to be a straightforward case of homegrown terrorism. A closer examination, however, raises questions. For example, Ayers was not a Muslim, did not have any connection to jihadist groups, and did not believe that he was acting on their behalf. He was a mentally troubled, poorly educated individual with, reportedly, sadistic tendencies, and he was upset at losing his girlfriend. None of this would preclude him from being labeled a terrorist. However, his motive may not have been political but rather to frighten the local drug dealers who he believed had gotten him hooked on methamphetamines. To disguise his involvement, he wanted to blame the bombings on jihadists. Again, none of this excuses his crimes, but should his actions count as terrorism? And if an individual tries to falsely blame an attack on jihadist ter-

[23] Dan Sullivan, "Experts: One-Time Neo-Nazi Charged in Double Murder Has Autism, Schizophrenia," *Tampa Bay Times*, December 19, 2019.

[24] "Michigan Airport Stabbing Probed as 'Lone Wolf' Terrorist Attack, FBI Says," CBS News, June 22, 2017; "Montrealer Amor Ftouhi Charged in Michigan Airport Stabbing," *Montreal Gazette*, June 22, 2017; Andy Riga, "Alleged Montreal Terrorist Used Jungle Survival Knife to Stab Officer," *Montreal Gazette*, June 22, 2017; and Lauren del Valle, "Flint Airport Stabbing Suspect to Remain in Jail," CNN, June 28, 2017.

rorists, does that make it a jihadist terrorist attack? Ayers was convicted in federal court on bombing and firearm charges, not terrorism.[25]

On February 15, 2018, **Martin Ryan Farnsworth**, a 16-year-old student in St. George, Utah, replaced the American flag at his high school with an ISIS flag and tagged one of the school's walls with the warning, "ISIS is coming." On March 5, he brought an improvised explosive device to the school and placed it in the cafeteria. The device fizzled and smoked but did not detonate. Farnsworth, a U.S.-born citizen, has been portrayed as suffering from autism and being a target of bullying at the school. What is at issue in this case is whether there is a terrorism connection to his actions. He pleaded guilty to attempting to use an incendiary device to injure someone and was sentenced to 415 days in a juvenile detention center, plus four years of probation. He was not considered to be a jihadist.[26]

It is unlikely that all readers will agree with all of my decisions to include or exclude certain individuals from the list of jihadist terrorists. Frankly, I myself went back and forth several times in some of the cases, and I am still not sure. That is the point. I describe the cases here, both inclusions and omissions, to illustrate the difficulty of deciphering motives, which is probably why experienced prosecutors want to steer clear of motivation and focus on whether the defendant carried out the act.

---

[25] Nikie Mayo, "Man Arrested During Probe of Suspicious Packages in Anderson Linked to Letters of 'Jihad,'" *Independent Mail*, March 8, 2018; Carla Field, "Federal Grand Jury Indicts Upstate Man Accused of Planting Explosives in Teddy Bear, Elsewhere," WYFF News, April 11, 2018; and U.S. Department of Justice, "Anderson Man Pleads Guilty in Federal Court to Using Weapons of Mass Destruction," press release, October 29, 2018c.

[26] Jessica Miller, "A Utah Teen Who Admitted to Bringing a Bomb to School Will Be on a Strict Probation for the Next 4 Years," *Salt Lake Tribune*, April 25, 2019.

References

10tv, "CBS Confirms Machete Attack Suspect Was in United States on Green Card," video clip, July 21, 2017.

Almasy, Steve, and Chuck Johnston, "Florida Teen Held in Killing Was Being Investigated by FBI over Possible ISIS Interest," CNN, March 15, 2018.

"American Volunteers Entered World War I Early," Voice of America, February 18, 2015.

Anderson, Curt, "FBI: No Foreign Terror Links in Florida Mall Bomb Plot," Associated Press, October 26, 2017.

Barker, Kim, Joseph Goldstein, and Michael Schwirtz, "Finding a Rootless Life in U.S., Sayfullo Saipov Turned to Radicalism," *New York Times*, November 1, 2017.

Batrawy, Aya, Paisley Dodds, and Lori Hinnant, "Leaked Isis Documents Reveal Recruits Have Poor Grasp of Islamic Faith," *The Independent*, August 16, 2016.

Bauman, Kurt J., and Nikki L. Graf, *Educational Attainment: 2000*, Washington, D.C.: U.S. Census Bureau, Census 2000 Brief, August 2003.

Bell, Stewart, "Sentencing Delayed for Canadian Who Plotted ISIS Attack as Defence Prepares Medical Reports," *Global News*, February 13, 2018.

Boutin, Bérénice, Grégory Chauzal, Jessica Dorsey, Marjolein Jegerings, Christophe Paulussen, Johanna Pohl, Alastair Reed, and Sofia Zavagli, *The Foreign Fighters Phenomenon in the European Union: Profiles, Threats & Policies*, The Hague: International Centre for Counter-Terrorism, April 2016.

Callimachi, Rukmini, and Catherine Porter, "Toronto Shooting Rekindles Familiar Debate: Terrorist? Mentally Ill? Both?" *New York Times*, July 25, 2018.

Carissimo, Justin, "FBI: Man Planned ISIS-Inspired Christmas Day Terror Attack in San Francisco," CBS News, December 22, 2017.

Chavez, Nicole, "What We Know About the New York Attack," CNN, November 1, 2017a.

———, "Pennsylvania Police Shootings Were 'Terror Attack,' DHS Says," CNN, December 24, 2017b.

Chittum, Matt, "Wasil Farat Farooqui to Serve 16 Years for Knife Attack That Drew National Attention," *Roanoke Times*, January 23, 2018.

Circuit Court of Cook County (Ill.), appeal of the conviction of Nomad Khan, No. 1-15-0731, March 14, 2017. As of June 8, 2020:
https://courts.illinois.gov/r23_orders/AppellateCourt/2017/1stDistrict/1150731_R23.pdf

Collin County (Tex.) Magistrate, affidavit for arrest warrant for Matin Azizi-Yarand, Warrant No. 18-136, April 30, 2018. As of June 8, 2020:
https://www.collincountytx.gov/public_information/news/PublishingImages/Azizi-Yarand%20Terrostic%20Threat%20Affidavit.pdf

Comey, James B., "Threats to the Homeland," testimony presented before the Senate Committee on Homeland Security and Governmental Affairs, Washington, D.C.: U.S. Department of Justice, October 8, 2015.

Crain, Caleb, "Lost Illusions: The Americans Who Fought in the Spanish Civil War," *New Yorker*, April 11, 2016.

del Valle, Lauren, "Flint Airport Stabbing Suspect to Remain in Jail," CNN, June 28, 2017.

Detman, Gary, "Police: Teen Confesses to Stabbings, Converted to Islam," KCBY News, March 13, 2018.

Dienst, Jonathan, "Number of Americans Trying to Join ISIS Doubles in a Year: Department of Justice," NBC New York, September 30, 2015.

Disaster Center, "United States Crime Rates, 1960–2018," webpage, undated. As of July 1, 2020:
http://www.disastercenter.com/crime/uscrime.htm

Donnelly, Maria Galperin, Thomas M. Sanderson, and Zack Fellman, *Foreign Fighters in History*, Washington, D.C.: Center for Strategic and International Studies, 2017.

Donnelly, Maria Galperin, Thomas M. Sanderson, Olga Oliker, Maxwell B. Markusen, and Denis Sokolov, "Russian-Speaking Foreign Fighters in Iraq and Syria," Center for Strategic and International Studies, December 29, 2017.

Dunigan, Jonece Starr, "Citizen Tip Leads to Arrest of Man Facing Terrorism Charge in Huntsville," AL.com, March 6, 2019.

Dworkin, Anthony, *Beyond Good and Evil: Why Europe Should Bring ISIS Foreign Fighters Home*, London: European Council on Foreign Relations, October 25, 2019.

Ellis, Ralph, "Terror Attack at San Francisco's Pier 39 Thwarted, Federal Authorities Say," CNN, December 23, 2017.

English, Stephen, "'Fire Where You Hear Screams'—ISIS-Inspired Teen Allegedly Considered Other Targets," *Fort Worth Star-Telegram*, May 3, 2018.

Europol, *TE-SAT: European Union Terrorism Situation and Trend Report*, The Hague, 2018.

FBI—*See* Federal Bureau of Investigation.

"FBI: Florida Man Sympathized with Islamic State, Wanted to Bomb Mall," CBS News, October 23, 2017.

Federal Bureau of Investigation, *Terrorism 2002–2005*, Washington, D.C.: U.S. Department of Justice, 2006. As of June 10, 2019:
https://www.fbi.gov/stats-services/publications/terrorism-2002-2005

Ferrise, Adam, and Eric Heisig, "Cleveland Terrorism Suspect's Penchant for Violence Stretches Nearly 30 Years," Cleveland.com, January 30, 2019.

Field, Carla, "Federal Grand Jury Indicts Upstate Man Accused of Planting Explosives in Teddy Bear, Elsewhere," WYFF News, April 11, 2018.

Frank, BrieAnna J., and Uriel J. Garcia, "18-Year-Old Shot by Deputy and Charged with Terrorism Released from Jail Prior to Trial," *Arizona Republic*, October 4, 2019.

Furst, Randy, "Man Sentenced to 15 Years for ISIS-Inspired Knife Attack at Mall of America," *Star Tribune*, February 16, 2018.

Herskovitz, Jon, "Honduras Man Living in Miami Charged with Trying to Bomb a Mall," Reuters, October 23, 2017.

Hochshield, Adam, *Spain in Our Hearts: Americans in the Spanish Civil War, 1936–1939*, New York: Houghton Mifflin Harcourt, 2016.

Horner, Sarah, "Health Issues Delay Trial for Former Student Accused of Setting Fires at St. Catherine University," *Pioneer Press*, January 25, 2019.

International Center for the Study of Violent Extremism, "About Breaking the ISIS Brand," webpage, undated. As of June 20, 2019:
https://www.icsve.org/about-breaking-the-isis-brand/

"ISIS Publicly Beheads Its Fighters for Desertion: Report," NDTV, January 31, 2016.

"Islamic State Follower Seeks Lower Bond in Officer Assault Case," AZCentral.com, September 5, 2019.

Jenkins, Brian Michael, *The Border War: A Study of United States-Mexico Relations During the Mexican Revolution 1910–1920*, Los Angeles, Calif.: University of California at Los Angeles, master's thesis, 1964.

———, "Going Jihad: The Fort Hood Slayings and Home-Grown Terrorism," testimony presented before the Senate Homeland Security and Governmental Affairs Committee on November 19, 2009, Santa Monica, Calif.: RAND Corporation, CT-336, 2009. As of June 10, 2019:
https://www.rand.org/pubs/testimonies/CT336.html

———, *Stray Dogs and Virtual Armies: Radicalization and Recruitment to Jihadist Terrorism in the United States Since 9/11*, Santa Monica, Calif.: RAND Corporation, OP-343-RC, 2011. As of June 10, 2019:
https://www.rand.org/pubs/occasional_papers/OP343.html

———, *When Jihadis Come Marching Home: The Terrorist Threat Posed by Westerners Returning from Syria and Iraq*, Santa Monica, Calif.: RAND Corporation, PE-130-1-RC, 2014. As of June 10, 2019:
https://www.rand.org/pubs/perspectives/PE130-1.html

———, *Inspiration, Not Infiltration: Jihadist Conspirators in the United States*, testimony presented before the House Oversight and Governmental Reform Committee on December 10, 2015, Santa Monica, Calif.: RAND Corporation, CT-447, 2015. As of June 10, 2019:
https://www.rand.org/pubs/testimonies/CT447.html

———, *The Origins of America's Jihadists*, Santa Monica, Calif.: RAND Corporation, PE-251-RC, 2017. As of June 10, 2019:
https://www.rand.org/pubs/perspectives/PE251.html

Jenkins, Brian Michael, and Jean-François Clair, *Trains, Concert Halls, Airports, and Restaurants—All Soft Targets: What the Terrorist Campaign in France and Belgium Tells Us About the Future of Jihadist Terrorism in Europe*, San Jose, Calif.: Mineta Transportation Institute, 2016.

Johnson, Scott, "Minnesota Man Explains Mall Stabbings," *Power Line* blog, January 28, 2018. As of June 10, 2020:
https://www.powerlineblog.com/archives/2018/01/minnesota-man-explains-mall-stabbings.php

King, Michael, "Suspect in Restaurant Machete Attack Was on FBI's Radar," WCMH-TV, February 2016.

Kleinberg, Eliot, "New: BallenIsles Killer Had Unsteady Family Life, from Missouri to Florida," *Palm Beach Post*, March 16, 2018.

Knuth, Sara, "Man Who Stabbed Cañon City Police Department Officer Sentenced," *Cañon City Daily Record*, April 15, 2019.

Mannix, Andy, "Psychologist: Suspect in St. Kate's Terror Case Now Competent to Face Charges," *Star Tribune*, December 20, 2019.

Markovitzky, Yaacov, *Machal: Overseas Volunteers in Israel's War of Independence*, Jerusalem: Israeli Ministry of Education, 2007. As of June 12, 2019:
https://www.mahal-idf-volunteers.org/about/Machal.pdf

Mayo, Nikie, "Man Arrested During Probe of Suspicious Packages in Anderson Linked to Letters of 'Jihad,'" *Independent Mail*, March 8, 2018.

McKay, Hollie, "Almost All American ISIS Fighters Are Unaccounted For," *New York Post*, October 27, 2017.

Meleagrou-Hitchens, Alexander, Seamus Hughes, and Bennett Clifford, *The Travelers: American Jihadists in Syria and Iraq*, Washington, D.C.: George Washington University, February 2018.

"Michigan Airport Stabbing Probed as 'Lone Wolf' Terrorist Attack, FBI Says," CBS News, June 22, 2017.

Miller, Jessica, "A Utah Teen Who Admitted to Bringing a Bomb to School Will Be on a Strict Probation for the Next 4 Years," *Salt Lake Tribune*, April 25, 2019.

Mogato, Manuel, "Philippines Doctor Linked to New York Attack Plot a 'Regular, Generous Guy,'" Reuters, October 10, 2017.

Mohamed, Besheer, and Elizabeth Podrebarac Sciupac, "The Share of Americans Who Leave Islam Is Offset by Those Who Become Muslim," Pew Research Center, January 26, 2018.

"Montrealer Amor Ftouhi Charged in Michigan Airport Stabbing," *Montreal Gazette*, June 22, 2017.

Mordock, Jeff, "Ohio Man Accused of Plotting Terror Attack on Cleveland July 4th Parade," *Washington Times*, July 2, 2018.

Morris, Loveday, and Mustafa Salim, "A File on Islamic State's 'Problem' Foreign Fighters Shows Some Are Refusing to Fight," *Washington Post*, February 7, 2017.

Mueller, John, "What Happened to the Islamic State Foreign Fighters That Had Returned to Europe?" *National Interest,* November 5, 2018.

National Commission on Terrorist Attacks upon the United States, *The 9/11 Commission Report*, Washington, D.C., 2004.

National Counterterrorism Center, *Foreign Terrorist Inspired, Enabled, and Directed Attacks in the United States Since 9/11*, McLean, Va., January 2019, Not available to the general public.

Nelson, Tim, "Man Charged in Mall of America Stabbing Previously Committed to State Psychiatric Care," Minnesota Public Radio, November 15, 2017.

New America, "Terrorism in America After 9/11—Part II: Who Are the Terrorists?" Washington, D.C., undated. As of June 8, 2020: https://www.newamerica.org/in-depth/terrorism-in-america/who-are-terrorists

"New York Truck Attack: Who Is Suspect Sayfullo Saipov?" BBC News, November 2, 2017.

Osborne, Mark, and Ben Stein, "Pennsylvania Cop Shooting Suspect's 'A Chicken, Not a Terrorist': Ex-Brother-in-Law," ABC News, December 24, 2017.

Owens, Bob, "Mexican Revolution and the Role Played by Tijuana," *San Diego Reader*, February 25, 1988.

Petska, Alicia, "Roanoke County Stabbing Suspect Came Under FBI Investigation After 2016 Trip to Turkey," *Roanoke Times*, August 14, 2017.

Pew Research Center, *America's Changing Religious Landscape*, Washington D.C., May 12, 2015.

"Police Try to Trace Steps of Suspect in NYC Attack," CBS News, December 11, 2017.

Pond, Allison, and Greg Smith, "The 'Zeal of the Convert': Is It the Real Deal?" Pew Research Center, October 28, 2009.

"Port Authority Explosion: What We Know About Suspect Akayed Ullah," CBS News, December 11, 2017.

Pulkkinen, Levi, "Jewish Federation Killer Gets Life Without Parole Plus 120 Years," *Seattle PI*, January 13, 2010.

Remkus, Ashley, "Alabama College Student Sentenced to 15 Years in Federal Prison for ISIS Bombing Plot," AL.com, March 7, 2019.

Riga, Andy, "Alleged Montreal Terrorist Used Jungle Survival Knife to Stab Officer," *Montreal Gazette*, June 22, 2017.

Rippy, J. Fred, "Mexican Projects of the Confederates," *Southwestern Historical Quarterly*, Vol. 22, No. 4, April 1919, pp. 291–317.

"Seattle Shooting Suspect Grew Distant from Kin," NBC News, July 31, 2006.

Siberell, Justin, "Country Reports on Terrorism 2015," special briefing, Washington, D.C.: U.S. Department of State, June 2, 2016. As of June 12, 2019: https://2009-2017.state.gov/r/pa/prs/ps/2016/06/258013.htm

"St. Catherine Arson Spree Shows Difficulty in Predicting Terror Attacks," CBS Minnesota, February 17, 2018.

Stavridis, Terry, "The Greek-Americans and Balkan Wars 1912–13: Helping the Old Homeland," *Macedonian Studies Journal*, Vol. 1, No. 2, 2014, pp. 133–162.

Stelloh, Tim, "'It Was Chaos': Victim Describes Brutal Machete Attack at Ohio Restaurant," NBC News, February 22, 2016.

Sullivan, Dan, "Experts: One-Time Neo-Nazi Charged in Double Murder Has Autism, Schizophrenia," *Tampa Bay Times*, December 19, 2019.

Sullivan, Jennifer, "'You Should Be Proud,' Haq Told Mother After Shootings," *Seattle Times*, November 5, 2009.

"Suspect Accused of Stabbing Officer Showed Interest in Terrorism," KKTV News, December 9, 2014.

Tracy, Erin, "'Ready to Die': Modesto Man Suspect in Planned Christmas Attack in San Francisco," *Modesto Bee*, December 23, 2017.

Tucker, Eric, "FBI: Shooter at Pensacola Navy Base Coordinated with al-Qaida," *Military Times*, May 18, 2020.

Tyree, Elizabeth, and Annie Andersen, "Man Connected to 'ISIS-Inspired' Knife Attack in Roanoke Co. Sentenced to 16 Years," WSET News, January 23, 2018.

Uenuma, Francine, "During the Mexican-American War, Irish-Americans Fought for Mexico in the 'Saint Patrick's Battalion,'" *Smithsonian Magazine*, March 15, 2019.

"Update: Farooqui Sentenced to Serve 16 Years for Double Stabbing," WDBJ News, January 23, 2018.

U.S. Census Bureau, "Educational Attainment in the United States: 2019," webpage, March 30, 2020. As of July 1, 2020:
https://www.census.gov/data/tables/2019/demo/educational-attainment/cps-detailed-tables.html

U.S. Code, Title 18, Section 249, Hate Crime Acts, October 28, 2009.

U.S. Code, Title 18, Section 2331, Definitions, October 3, 2018.

U.S. Department of Justice, "Charges Unsealed Against Three Men for Plotting to Carry Out Terrorist Attacks in New York City for ISIS in the Summer of 2016," press release, October 6, 2017.

———, "Alabama Man Sentenced to 15 Years in Prison for Attempting to Provide Material Support to ISIS," press release, June 20, 2018a.

———, "Ohio Man Arrested for Attempting to Assist a Foreign Terrorist Organization with Homeland Attack Plot," press release, July 2, 2018b.

———, "Anderson Man Pleads Guilty in Federal Court to Using Weapons of Mass Destruction," press release, October 29, 2018c.

———, "California Man Arrested in Terror Plot to Detonate Explosive Device Designed to Kill Innocents," press release, April 29, 2019.

U.S. District Court for the Northern District of Ohio, criminal complaint against Demetrius Pitts, Case No. 1:18 MJ 2120, July 2, 2018. As of June 8, 2020:
https://www.justice.gov/opa/press-release/file/1077151/download

Wang, Amy B, "FBI Thwarts Alleged Plan to Carry Out Terrorist Attack in San Francisco on Christmas," *Washington Post*, December 23, 2017.

———, "A Teen with Former Neo-Nazi Ties Claims His 'Muslim Faith' Led Him to Stab Three, Police Say," *Washington Post*, March 22, 2018.

Wigglesworth, Valerie, "Plano Teen Arrested in ISIS-Inspired Plot to Commit Mass Shooting at Frisco's Stonebriar Mall," *Dallas Morning News*, May 2, 2018.

Williams, Heather J., Nathan Chandler, and Eric Robinson, *Trends in the Draw of Americans to Foreign Terrorist Organizations from 9/11 to Today,* Santa Monica, Calif.: RAND Corporation, RR-2545-OSD, 2018. As of June 12, 2019: https://www.rand.org/pubs/research_reports/RR2545.html

Winton, Richard, "L.A. Suspect in Terror Plot Lived Quiet Life but Spewed Online Hate, Authorities Say," *Los Angeles Times*, April 30, 2019.

Winton, Richard, and James Queally, "L.A. Terror Plot Thwarted: Army Vet Planned 'Mass Casualties,' FBI Says," *Los Angeles Times*, April 29, 2019.

Xiong, Chao, "Former St. Catherine University Student Capable of Understanding Terrorism Charges, Doctor Testifies," *Star Tribune*, November 2, 2018.

About the Author

Brian Michael Jenkins is a senior adviser to the president at the RAND Corporation and author of numerous books, reports, and articles on terrorism-related topics. In addition, he is a research associate at the Mineta Transportation Institute, where he directs the continuing research on protecting surface transportation against terrorist attacks. Jenkins holds a master's degree in history.